Writing Handbooks

Writing
for
Soaps

Chris Curry

A & C Black • London

First published 2002
A & C Black Publishers Limited
37 Soho Square, London W1D 3QZ
www.acblack.com

ISBN 0–7136–6121–6

A CIP catalogue record for this book is available from
the British Library.

A & C Black uses paper produced with elemental
chlorine-free pulp, harvested from managed
sustainable forests.

Typeset in $10\frac{1}{2}$ on $12\frac{1}{2}$ pt Sabon
Printed and bound in Great Britain by
Creative Print and Design (Wales), Ebbw Vale

The publishers are grateful to Simon Frith and the
BBC for giving their permission to reproduce an
extract from *The Archers*.

Writing Handbooks

Writing
for
Soaps

Contents

Introduction...

... Quickly followed, in many a Soap writer's experience, by: Really! But what's your proper job?

Okay, so it hasn't single-handedly replaced coal and steel, but television is a serious industry and Soap one of its most successful products. As a genre, Soap Opera started its life in the United States. As broadcast serialised drama it got the first half of its name from the fact that soap manufacturers sponsored it, and the second part from 'opera buffa', which is a comic opera with characters drawn from everyday life. By now, Soap has become the generic term for popular drama that:

(a) deals mainly with domestic themes;
(b) is centred around the lives of a set gallery of characters;
(c) is broadcast or transmitted on a regular, ongoing basis.

Over the last decade, not only have several new British Soaps appeared but old stalwarts have increased their episode output by as much as sevenfold. In what may be only the first example of reincarnation, one particular Soap that had been deemed to have run its course has been brought back to our screens. The Soap genre has now become so much a part of our popular culture that it has not only spawned its own rack of dedicated fanzines but also become the subject of much learned debate. In the tabloid press, Soap stars can command as much interest as royalty and hardly a month goes by when some broadsheet isn't airing a view on the influence that Soap may or may not be having on our modern-day society.

At the time of writing, the British viewing public devours some 36 hours or so of Soap a week (of which around 15½ are home-grown), while those willing to shell out more than the

1

licence fee are free to feast on another 56 hours of ongoing drama. And every moment of it has to be written.

Many an ambition to become a Soap scriptwriter is born of a desire to be involved with a particular, personally regarded series. Admirable. Some aspire to write for any Soap, honourably, but with a weather-eye on Soap's rare ability to deliver what other markets cannot – huge audiences, regular employment and respectable financial rewards. Understandable. If you've ever constituted a third of the audience at a wet Wednesday matinee fringe performance of your painfully wrought two-hander, fretting less about the structure of the second half than whether the proceeds will cover the tube fare home, you could be forgiven for thinking there must be a more rewarding writerly row to hoe.

Others see Soap scribing as a relatively undemanding way of earning enough to finance the finer things they want to write. Show me a writer who hasn't suspected they might be Booker material if only they could buy themselves the luxury of enough real writing time, and I'll show you a caring estate-agent! And speaking of the unashamedly cynical… There are writers who are more rancorous about Soap than the most savage critic could ever be and proud of the fact that this doesn't stop them writing it. Soap, as they see it, is just something to put between the ads. And writing any old wallpaper that the thicko masses will sit and watch is something they happily condescend to do – just as long as they can laugh all the way to the building society.

None of the above motives for wanting to script Soap precludes people from doing it. If there was any justice, the basest of them would stop people doing it well. But there isn't and it doesn't. All of the above do, however, carry Health Warnings. But more of that later (*see* Chapter 9).

However noble or not their callings, what all Soap writers must have in common is the knack of practising some pretty specific skills. Even when they have experience in other fields, writers can find that Soap calls for a whole new box of tricks. Some of these skills may need to be brought into play before the actual business of writing begins, which is where this guide may differ from those dealing purely with writing technique. For instance, on those Soaps where the writer is expected to be a part of the storylining process, their inventiveness, their performance at planning meetings and their ability to cope with the collaborative nature of the job in general may be almost as crucial as their performance on the page. So, although not dealing with writing *per se*, the chapter on storyline meetings is relevant to the Soap-writing process.

After describing what is expected of a Soap writer and offering some tips on how to get started, the body of this book effectively falls into three main sections:

- The first has already been mentioned, and covers the start of the creative process by exploring the different degrees of influence that the Soap writer might have over stories and plotlines.
- The second section gets down to the actual creation of a script and, although Chapters 3 and 4 deal with construction, presentation and dialogue, Chapters 5, 6 and 7 also discuss Soap-specific elements that the writer will need to take into consideration. For any Very New Writers I've tried to cover some writing basics as well as those specific to Soap writing as we follow the process of script creation through. Most or all of this the more seasoned will already know, but – writers being a fairly generous lot, on the whole – I can only rely on them to bear with me and remember when they didn't know their POVs from a Plum Duff.
- The final section (Sample Storyline and Sample Script) is intended to demonstrate the whole by putting into practice all that has been discussed along the way. This section offers the writer new to Soap the chance to try their hand at creating part or all of a Soap script for themselves.

Since comparisons are odious and castigation is alive and well in the review section of every Sunday supplement, I intend to keep opinion on the state of current Soap output general and down to a dull roar. This is not just because I am indebted to Soap for the living I made from writing it for many years, or out of respect for the writers I know who are still doing it. It is because, frankly, to criticise the content of the Soap phenomenon in the kind of depth it warrants would be a whole other book. This one is not about the relative merits of our Soaps, nor is it an analysis of whether the quality as a whole justifies us being as dedicated to them as we are. It's not about *why* Soap gets onto our screens – more one writer's glimpse into *how*.

1. The Soap Writer's Remit

Before we get on to what's involved in the process of bringing a Soap to the screen, and to the specifics of writing a script, aspiring Soap writers will no doubt be encouraged to know that there are no particular qualifications (formal or otherwise) required for the job. There is, however, one basic quality that no Soap writer, no matter how talented, can do without – stamina.

As with all other forms of writing, what separates those who do it from those who don't is as much to do with tenacity as it is with talent. Writing of any sort, whether it be the novel, the play, the poem or whatever, is an act of communication. It helps if you have a need to communicate; it's even more of a bonus if you have an innate bent for being able to do it or the ability to learn the skill. However, none of that will matter a row of beans if you balk at the idea of hard graft.

Having a good idea for a book, film, poem or play is the fun part. Some people's energy and enjoyment may even sustain through the first chapter, scene or stanza, but there soon comes the point at which they realise that they're gambolling on the foothills and where they must get to is the top of K2. If the writing challenge that was undertaken was for an unsolicited piece of work, it doesn't matter to anyone but the writer if they decide to abandon the attempt or put the piece aside for a while in favour of the next engaging idea. However, Soap – more than any other writing remit – does not allow for writers to do anything other than finish the job they have been commissioned to start and within a strictly allotted time. In television accountancy terms, the reason why Soaps are so popular is that they are relatively cheap to produce. To maintain this cost-effectiveness Soaps must run like well-oiled machines, which means that there is no time to indulge anyone involved in the process – including the writers.

In the Introduction I began with a reference to the proper job aspersion. Now we've established that Soap is just about as arduous a writing job as you're likely to get, we can move on to the next most frequently asked question that Soap writers tend to be asked about their remit.

Do you write all the episodes yourself?

The simple answer is no. As anyone who has done any writing will be aware – and as those who have no earthly reason to know – a very few minutes of what is seen on the screen takes a good deal longer than that to write. No single writer, no matter how fast, greedy or suicidal, could keep pace with the output of even a once-weekly half-hour of drama, let alone a twice or thrice weekly.

Unlike sit-com – or any other half-hour of television I can think of – Soap Opera never sleeps. There is no hibernation during the autumn schedules and no rest for the remainder of the year. The very nature of Soap is that it is as seamless and ongoing as any other slice of the viewers' lives. So multiply, say, three episodes a week – which can take between two and three weeks, or in some cases two or three months, to write – by a relentless 52 weeks of the year and you have a mathematical, let alone a physical, impossibility.

So which of the characters do *you* write for, then?

This is the third of the most frequently asked questions, and the answer is all of them. On most Soaps the writer produces the entire episode containing every word that comes out of each and every character's mouth. Every pearl of wisdom and practically every glottal stop is on the page along with more or less every move they make, and certainly every vow they break. Which is one of the reasons the scripts take as long as they do to write.

Team work

To cope with the colossal output, the majority of long-running Soaps employ a regular team of writers. Numbering anywhere between several and several dozen, these chosen few are sometimes also referred to collectively as 'a stable'. But then you'd hardly expect me to subscribe to this particular description, given the pejorative leap you've probably already made to do with hacks!

Getting onto the team

Writers tend to get picked to write Soap for one of half-a-dozen reasons:

- Their agent has put them forward as a candidate.
- They have already had some work produced and the Script Editor has spotted them as a potential writing-team member.
- They have a mate already on the writing team who has enough faith in their talent (proven in production or not) to recommend them.
- They have a mate already on the team who owes them one.
- They have a mate already on the team who knows that The-Powers-That-Be are looking for a new writer and would prefer it to be the devil they know.

Or – and this can and does happen – they know nobody, they've no track-record whatsoever, and yet the unsolicited script they submitted makes the script editor or producer think they might just fit the bill. In my own case, I had written some radio drama before a friend put a word in for me on a Soap, but I have worked alongside writers who had had nothing previously published or broadcast before being accepted onto a Soap-writing team.

Notes for new writers

There's no point in pretending that it is common for untested writers to sail straight onto a Soap-writing team. However, as with trying to break into any other writing field, there is only one way: to put your work out there and risk it being ignored or rejected in the hope that your potential may – just may – be recognised and seized upon.

Getting a Soap start

If you have no agent or mates already in the business, but believe that you can fulfil the remit and become a successful

Soap writer, you will need to prove it by submitting a piece of work that shows your potential. Since there is a league-table of Soaps – to do with audience figures and not necessarily quality of output, I hasten to add – it is probably sensible for a wholly untried writer to begin by approaching the less high-profile Soaps with samples of work. Should you be successful and get commissioned, there is no doubt that learning your trade at the modest end of the spectrum will stand you in better stead when it comes to applying to write for those fighting to maintain their lofty championship status. In fact, once a writer has gained some grounding by writing for a Soap, it is not unknown for them to be approached – not to say poached – by bigger-budget, larger-audience-grabbing shows.

What to submit

But back to the reality of getting someone to recognise your ability in the first place. In terms of what kind of material you should submit, this varies from show to show. In the case of some Soaps, *Eastenders* among them, Script Department advice is that wannabe writers should submit anything *but* a 'pretend' or 'dummy' episode. This is on the basis that there are so many in-house conventions for the aspiring writer to unwittingly trip over; so many cardinal rules for them to inadvertently break that it's hard for them to give a novice's script a fair reading.

While some script readers have a disinclination for submissions based on their particular show, what they *are* actively seeking is a demonstration of the writer's instinct for Soap writing in the general sense. To illustrate that you possess this instinct it makes sense to submit a piece of writing that is at least as long as the episode transmission time of the programme you are seeking to write for. This invariably means 30 minutes for television Soaps and 15 minutes in radio episode time for *The Archers*.

Yet more crucially than proving you can go the distance, the sample of your work has to show an aptitude for creating and maintaining structure as well as demonstrating that you are able to successfully build to a series of emotional and/or narrative turning points. As one Script Editor put it, they get some 'lovely [unsolicited] writing, but . . . ' The 'but' being that however tender, moving or gritty a vignette can be, it won't cut any ice if it doesn't demonstrate a feeling for plot and pace.

Then again, some script readers quite definitely *do* like samples of work to be based on their own show. In the case of *The Archers*, for instance, the Editor's feeling is very much that she needs to know a writer has a talent to write for that particular show as opposed to any other show or indeed any other genre. To this end *The Archers* helpfully produce a Script Pack which contains some writing tips together with a dummy storyline on which aspiring writers can base their submission. This is available by writing to the BBC's Broadcasting Centre at Pebble Mill Road, Birmingham B5 7QQ. For those so keen to try their hand that they can't await the arrival of the Script Pack, *The Archers'* Editor recommends listening to an episode and then attempting to write the follow-on episode – *before*, she stresses, listening to the next one. This advice is based on the sound sense that it is virtually impossible for the aspiring writer to ignore the tack and tone that the next broadcast episode takes, when what the Editor and/or Producer will be trying to weigh is what your individual approach to the follow-up episode would have been.

In the case of *The Archers* a promising submission just may win you a place on a mock script-meeting day. This chance to show up in person is designed to sound writers out for a real and informed interest in matters rural and to give the Producer and Editor a general idea of how well the sort of storyline suggestions you might make would sit within the show's ethos. It's also an opportunity to meet and talk with one or more of the programme's regular writers and to hear first-hand the degree of commitment required – and since *The Archers'* schedule is an extremely fast-paced one it's as well to be aware of it from the outset. Should you appear to be the right stuff you may be given a further mock storyline to confirm how well you handle it in writing terms, or you may be fortunate enough to pass straight on to the reserve list of writers to await your first proper commission.

Channel 5's *Family Affairs* is another of the Soaps that welcomes submissions based on their show, and they also produce a sample Script Pack – available by writing to Channel 5, 22 Long Acre, London WC2E 9LY.

If you are uncertain as to what the preference is when it comes to unsolicited material for the particular show you are aiming at, you can always ring the programme's help-line if they have one or, if not, write to the Script Department to ask. Addresses and telephone numbers for the television and radio companies that produce Soaps can be found in *The Writers' & Artists' Yearbook* published by A & C Black or in the *Writer's Handbook* published by Macmillan. Even if you decide to take a flyer and submit what you think will grab their attention, it's not a bad idea to ring the show you're aiming at – *Eastenders*, for instance, do operate a help-line – to find out whose attention you are trying to grab. Television job designations can change fast and responsibility for the reading of unsolicited scripts is one of the jobs that tends to get handed around a lot on some Soaps, so it's probably worth phoning when you are ready to post off your offering to find out if there is someone more specific than the Producer or the Script Editor to whom you can direct your work. Where producers and script editors are concerned, taking a name from an on-screen list of credits at the end of your favoured show won't (for reasons that will become clear later) necessarily mean you will be aiming your work at someone *currently* doing those jobs. So it's worth the cost of a phone call to get up-to-date information.

Presenting unsolicited work

Whatever unsolicited material you are submitting as a new writer attempting to catch a Soap script-reader's eye, it's worth spending some time on *how* you should present it. Some further, more detailed notes on scene headings, stage directions, etc. appear in Chapter 4, but for now we will deal with the absolute basics of presentation. These are general points that should ideally be applied to any writing work you submit to potential markets.

• You may think it shouldn't, but it does matter that your script looks as competent as the writing it (hopefully) contains. Apart from simply making it easier for a busy producer or script editor to assess your ability, a well-presented attempt not only demonstrates your professionalism, but is a polite nod in the direction of theirs. Remember that whoever receives your script will invariably be deluged with material from other hopefuls, and that those offerings which shriek 'amateur' will be the last to be picked out of the pile or the first to be binned. After all, if you get a carelessly scrawled estimate from a builder, it suggests that you would get a carelessly executed job. Your submission should engender a sense of confidence in you from the outset. Overall, what you are aiming to present is a clean, clear script.

- Use a good-quality A4 paper and don't be tempted to economise by using both sides.

- Leave a margin of at least 4 cm on the left-hand side of the page and allow a generous margin on the right.

- Even if you were top of the class in calligraphy, it is never acceptable to submit a handwritten script. Always submit work that is typed or word-processed – even if it costs you a couple of bob and/or a sexual favour! If your keyboard skills are lousy, get practising. By submitting sample work to a Soap, you are applying for regular employment as a competent and reliable tradesperson. If you do land the job, deadlines will be tight and having to get someone else to type up your scripts will be a time-consuming and unnecessarily costly option.

- Although not specifically to do with the initial submission of your work, it's worth mentioning at this point that having writers deliver scripts and/or rewrites on disk or by email is becoming an increasingly popular option with Soap pro-gramme-makers. Given the pace at which schedules must move, the time and costs involved in land postage routes and the expense of arranging face-to-face meetings, it's hardly surprising that script editors have begun to choose this fast-track way of dealing with their writers. In other words, if you haven't already, it's time to master your technophobia – on the assumption that if you do find employment as a Soap writer, computer literacy will inevitably become a job require-ment if it isn't already a prerequisite. Again, you may be thinking that these nuts and bolts of script presentation and delivery shouldn't matter and that what should is the quality of the writing. To this fair point I can only respond with a brutal fact: although there are legions of talented writers, no more than a small percentage of the population make their living solely from writing. If it is your ambition to win regular, ongoing and lucrative writing work, it is in your own interests to arm yourself with every tool that might conceivably be required for the job.

- Before submitting any material, make double-double sure that your work is checked for spelling and typing errors. If, at this stage, you are working on a typewriter and need to make a tiny correction or two, make them as undetectable as possible. Work littered with biro scrawls over correction fluid is not a good introduction. It'll be hard to convince a script reader that you are capable of the kind of hard graft mentioned earlier as a Soap writer's prerequisite if they see that you couldn't even be bothered to re-type your work. When producing your material on a PC, print a hard copy and check for those spelling mistakes and literals that can somehow survive dozens of readings on the screen.

- When aiming your sample work at television Soaps, use double line spacing. For submissions to radio, the BBC's own guidelines recommend single line spacing with double space between speeches, but as their own in-house format is typed up with a one-and-a-half space between lines of dialogue, this would be acceptable.

- Always number the pages. You'd be surprised how many people don't bother and it does matter. The average script reader's desk can look like an explosion in a paper mill, and if un-numbered sections of a script get mixed up or separated there is no way that he or she will be spending time trying to put it back into sequence. Even if you staple all the pages of your submission together, it may well be that a script reader will want to separate out a scene or two to show to someone else. Should your script show enough promise to get you phoned or invited in to discuss it, page numbers will obviously come into their own when it comes to easy reference.

- Always keep a copy (hard or on disk) of any work you submit to anyone. Having had the benefit of this wise advice in my early writing days, I only once broke the rule. Desperate for time I posted six uncopied episodes of a radio series to my agent who was hopeful of a market for it – if we hit while the iron was hot. Several weeks' worth of hard work safely traversed the country only to be accidentally left on the tube by the agent who was taking it home to read. So sorry – and could I please just pop another copy in the post? I felt like the complete idiot that I was, having to admit that I didn't have another copy – and as unprofessional as you will feel when that script editor rings to say he was enjoying your script immensely up until the point where his hamster ate it, and could you please just pop another copy . . .

Familiarity breeds commission chances

This will be covered in more detail later on in the book, but knowing the Soap you have ambitions to write for is important from the outset, since it will obviously increase your chances if your unsolicited material is geared towards the show's particular characteristics.

Knowing the nuts and bolts

By nuts and bolts I mean the background mechanisms of timing and tone against which your chosen Soap operates. Making a study of these means that, even where you are not submitting a dummy script based on the specific programme, you can ensure that your offering allows glimpses of your ability to create and sustain the same sort of pace and dynamics.

If you have not been, in truth, the most avid of long-term fans, then do as much back-reference research as you can by way of the compilation novels and/or video compilations that some of the Soaps have produced over the years. Having got a sense of the show's past, make a serious study of its present output. Watch every episode (at least several months' worth) armed with pen and paper to jot down practicalities like the average number of scenes per episode, average size of cast list, etc., as well as any of the less quantifiable aspects that might strike you, such as the general rhythm, the tenor of humour the Soap tends to use, the ratio of high drama to the lighter side of storytelling and, in general, the overall tone it imparts. By getting this deeper sense of the show, you will be more likely to choose a submission piece from your repertoire or create one that will appeal to the mind-set of a script reader on a particular Soap.

Knowing the characters

When quizzing the *Family Affairs* Story Producer about what he considered to be the key attribute for anyone aspiring to write for his show, his answer was unequivocal: the most valuable writers are those who *know the characters*. A man after my own heart when it comes to believing that the best drama comes out of character. So it's obvious that any script you send winging his way should show that you have studied the people as much – if not more – than the show's brand of pace and plotting.

Even where the philosophy of a show is somewhat inverted to favour incident-led over character-led drama, the aspiring writer needs to demonstrate that they are capable of maintaining consistency when it comes to material for established central characters. It stands to reason that a character's personality dictates their dialogue, so you need to pay attention to their general established traits and sensibilites before trying to put words into their mouths. If you do not already know your chosen Soap's major characters well enough to be able to predict their likely actions and reactions to any given situation, follow them through at least a couple of months' worth of episodes and then draw up a short character analysis of each of them. It need only list broad characteristics, as in the following example:

Dolores:
Vulnerable. Generous. Highly strung. Tendency to take on too much. Impatient with procrastinators.
Desmond:
Optimistic. Confident. Outspoken. Competitive. Can be na ve.

By going to this minimal amount of trouble you could save your calling-card script from the most obvious blunders when it comes to character portrayal and motivation. Once you feel confident that you know how their individual natures would be likely to make them behave and respond, you can start to concentrate on how they communicate.

Chapter 4 includes some advice on how you can practise honing your listening abilities in order to be able to recognise and reproduce individual speech patterns.

'Scene' any good Soaps lately?

It's evident from watching any single episode of Soap that the scenes contained within it vary not only in length but also in tone and pace. It would make for either pretty tedious or overly taxing viewing if, even where scenes contained different characters, the content were to be served up as a succession of one-note segments.

The experienced Soap writer automatically bears this potential pitfall in mind as they plan and write their scenes, whereas the novice may need to make a study of the avoidance of monotony. Again, watching Soaps – and in particular the one you'd ideally like to write for – constitutes valuable homework. This time the exercise goes beyond totting up the number and duration of scenes to take note of variations in temperature and tempo.

There is, of course, no absolute formula for how the shades of light and dark are juxtaposed on any given show, but it is possible for the aspiring Soap writer to develop a feel for the sort of mix that a show favours. As you will inevitably find that the programme's overall tone and pace varies within a given timespan as well as specifically within episodes, depending on the light or heavy nature of the major storyline, it's a good idea to monitor episodes over a two- or three-month run. All it needs for you to build up a picture of the general episode structure is to make a note of the contrasting moods against a list of scene numbers. Noting the duration of the scenes will give you an idea of the average ratio between the heavier and lighter sides of episode content. Your monitoring sheet need be no more complicated than this:

Scene	Characters	Story	Mood	Duration (min)
1	Des/Dolores	Abortion row	Heavy	1
2	Col/Cath/Clive	Wedding plans	Light	2

As this is Soap, and other storylines will undoubtedly be crossing over or crashing into the main focus of almost every scene, you'll need to remember that it is only the dominant temperature of the primary story that you're trying to take.

When you think you've done enough monitoring to give you a feeling for how the average episode is orchestrated, video-tape any episode and use your notes as a template from which you can attempt to write your own version.

If you find during the course of your practice-writing that your scenes tend to be consistently shorter than the original, check (by way of your video of the original) that your version covers all the relevant information, plot points, emotional nuances and undercurrents the writer had contained in the transmitted version. If, on the other hand, you are constantly writing longer scenes, refer back to the tape again and ask yourself with as much honesty as you can muster how much of your version was superfluous. Of course, it's nigh on impossible to judge your own work, but where you are pleased enough with your four-minute ersatz scene to declare it superior to the original three-minute version, do at at least have the grace (and good Soap sense) to remember that what the characters and story gained on the roundabouts of your extended scene, another set of characters and story has lost on the swings and that, in reality, you would have had to justify such favouritism and neglect.

You can't get too familiar

In general, then, the better you know the show, the better your chances are of writing for it. But this tenet isn't purely to do with getting onto a Soap-writing team in the first place. As you will see when we come to the story-conference stage and, beyond that, the actual writing stage, having a grasp of both the show's history and more recent story trends will have entirely practical implications.

Pass the Perrier

As well as most probably calling for your attendance at regular story conferences, Soap sometimes offers the writer several more opportunities to down all the fizzy water and day-old Danish they can handle. The story conference, long-term planning meetings, commissioning meeting, first-draft meeting and writer-director meeting will all be covered in some detail in subsequent passages, but in outlining the remit it would be remiss of me not to mention that such meetings may well be seen as part of the Soap writer's job spec. Some shows do pay their writers' expenses and/or a fee for their attendance at some or all of these meetings but, financial considerations aside, they can account for a great deal of time over and above the time spent writing scripts.

Your writing worked for them – will you?

If – no, let's be positive and say *when* – the sample of your work has convinced a Soap script editor or producer that you are a potential writer for their show, they will invariably want to confirm your suitability by meeting you in person. Earlier I outlined what form this meeting would take on *The Archers*, and some television Soaps do operate a similar system of getting potential writers in to talk with or be talked to by the Producer and\or Script Editor as well as one or more of the show's veteran writers.

On other shows they may invite you in for an informal preliminary chat just to check that it isn't a case of you writing like an angel while being, in fact, a complete sociopath who would disrupt the rest of the writing team from day one in.

Another possible option is that they decide to throw you in at the deep end by inviting you to a story conference. These story conferences or storylining sessions can take different forms (described in the next chapter), but however the show is devised, what the Producer/Script Editor will be trying to glean at this stage is that you know and care about the programme you have applied to write for.

A chance to change your mind

During any of the above inductions you will get to know more about the individual show's structure as it affects the writers' job specification. What you are required to do, and the timespan in which you will be required to do it, will inevitably sound daunting – especially to the very new writer. In this new field of work where there hasn't been a chance to prove yourself, even the writer with a track record in some other genre is entitled to some private doubts about being equal to the Soap task. If the remit sounded more exciting than daunting then this perfectly natural degree of misgiving should disappear with the acceptance of your first script. If, however, you have serious suspicions that, for you, the Soap game may not be worth the candle, now is time to admit it to yourself – and to them. Not everyone enjoys Soap writing and one thing is for sure: if you are not suited to it, it will not suit itself to you. By whatever process a Soap maintains its output, it cannot alter or risk faltering to accommodate any individual involved – including the writer.

2. Once Upon a Story Conference

New kid on the block

The writer's first time at a story conference can be a daunting experience, faced – as they most probably will be – by a seemingly solid phalanx of regulars who have been through hell, high water and low ratings together.

As you will know if you are one already, or should know if you are trying to become one, writers rank alongside actors when it comes to being among the most insecure group of people on the planet. A strange hybrid species, writers tend to veer wildly between the sort of insular precocity needed to flog their singular slant on life and a craven desire to have it bought by one and all. A writer-friend of mine once said he couldn't leave a note out for the milkman without feeling the need for some feedback.

Newcomers to a Soap story conference would do well to keep this insecurity factor in mind if, on their first day, X spends the morning glaring sullenly across the table at them. It'll either be because you've unwittingly sat where he or she *always* sits, or because they are worried you might have been brought in to take their place in more ways than one. Even the welcoming ones will have suspicion lurking helplessly behind their smiles. Are you going to be better than them? Are you the 'new direction' the Producer's been threatening to find? And, if so, will you supplant their campaign-weary old bones? The team might well be desperate for the transfusion of some fresh young blood if, despite their best experienced efforts, the show's popularity has been dwindling; but it's naïve to expect their relief not to be tinged with resentment. We're all relieved to see the AA man, but that doesn't mean we like not having been able to fix the blessed thing ourselves.

A shiny new presence at a story conference can also have not just ego-rocking, but entirely practical implications. Unless someone has died, left, or been disappeared, another hungry writer at the table means that there are fewer commissions to go around.

Getting down to business

However uneasily or not they end up sitting together, the purpose of convening this happy-band or nervous-breakdown of writers is to plan a block of future episodes. Just how much or how little the writers have to do with the formulation of storylines, as opposed to the writing of scripts, determines the length and importance of the storyline meeting, and differs depending on the show.

Some Soaps are more 'writer-led' than others. Writer-led means just what it says: the writers play a crucial part in devising and plotting the storylines, with the Producer, naturally, having the ultimate say on what does or doesn't run. On writer-led Soaps a two-day meeting once a month to plan a block of 12 episodes is not unheard of. On other serials, the writers may have a certain amount of input – suggesting events, issues, etc. in a general sense – but the definitive way in which stories are plotted is given over to storyliners.

In some, the Producer and/or Executive Producer will have firm to absolutely concrete ideas about what stories they want their programme to tackle and in what way. Not that difficult a deal for the writer when these ideas offer them the chance to get their teeth into something gritty or groundbreaking; less savoury a prospect when the Producer's current obsession is with the social and economic consequences of the falling water table. Some may not even bother with a story conference as such at all, preferring instead to involve only the writer or writers they have already decided to commission.

These different approaches to storylining will, of course, present the writer with different starting points when it comes to the actual writing of the script. I will be picking up on this again later but, for now, we will look at the different types of storyline breakdowns that can emerge.

Storyline breakdowns

A writer who has been offered a commission to write a script will almost certainly be supplied with some sort of storyline breakdown or story document to work from.

When it comes to writer-led shows, the storylines they had a hand in suggesting and plotting will be tidied up by the script editor(s) or story editor(s) into a loosely described set of events to occur within an episode. In this case the order in which scenes happen will not necessarily have been prescribed. It will be up to the writer to structure the episode as and when they come to tackle the job of writing it. On *The Archers*, for instance, there are no storyliners as such. After a story meeting where the Editor, Producer and writers all pitch in individual ideas for enhancement and development by the group as a whole, breakdowns are then knocked into episode shape by the Editor and Producer and issued to the writers. These script notes are detailed as to the story content of the episode but leave the writer a free hand when it comes to scene structure. The sample storyline given later as a template for the sample script (*see* Chapter 10) is an example of the sort of breakdown format that allows the writer to create structure as well as dialogue.

Where there are people whose specific job it is to storyline, the writer may be presented with a very tightly constructed template for the episode they have been asked to write. The number and sequence of scenes may be dictated, with the characters and events within each scene already sketched, as in the following example:

Sc. 998.01   INT.   DOG & DUCK PUB   DAY
GEMMA enters the empty bar to open up. JIM follows carrying crate of bottles. They grumble about how late the brewery deliveries are getting. As GEMMA unlocks the door, CAROL comes bursting through it and tells them that JOE has been taken to hospital.

Where the skeleton of stories and events has been so clearly predefined, the writer's job is seen as putting flesh on the bones of the characters by producing dialogue that will give substance and validity to the episode's events.

Which sort of template works?

They both work, and since I promised to keep value judgements down a minimum I won't dwell on my own view as to which of these methods results in the best-quality product. What does appear to be happening is that the writer-led scenario is becoming less common, while the predilection among producers is increasingly for handing down an already devised set of storylines, most of which are based on events or issues rather than on character.

As a Soap writer, it's down to you to decide whether you relish the responsibility of being given enough creative rope to plait into stuff of substance – or to hang yourself with – or whether you positively welcome being asked (as, I promise you, one producer put it) to just 'join up the dots'.

Story conference or Culloden?

It is debatable whether ruling writers out at the conception stage results in a screenful of amorphous creatures plodding through predictable plotlines. What can be argued is that less involvement at the storyline-meeting stage leads to a much quieter life.

A roomful of writers (*collect. a rabble*) under pressure to come up with yet another set of Soap happenings can end up generating a lot more heat than light and a deal more incitement than excitement. Where there are several thrown together of opposite sexes, different religions, opposing political views, various social backgrounds and diametrically opposed moral standpoints, it's not unknown for the whole thing to disintegrate into a common brawl over the question of a mythical character's motivation or the viability of one storyline idea over another.

When not resembling a war-zone, there are times when a stranger could be forgiven for thinking they have blundered into a particularly distressing group therapy session. To witness the inmates swapping their real-life personal miseries in an attempt to get their storyline idea elected is not a pretty sight. *'Believe me, I've been there, and having a little sister with brain-damage is worse than having an older brother with Aids. There's loads more mileage in it!'*

Whether the story conference is the Culloden kind or a civilised swap-shop of ideas, cracking how to cope with it

20

doesn't, of course, mean a writer is capable of producing the goods when it comes to penning the scripts. But since storylining isn't just a part, but the start of the process on most major shows, the better a writer does it, generally speaking, the better they'll do.

Conference tactics

As with any team, especially one made up of creative neurotics, egos are everywhere, hurts are historic and politics complicated, and there are those who either never manage or quickly decide they don't want to infiltrate. Others may relish the cut-and-thrust – and the company, since writing is usually so solitary a game. If you do decide to hang in there, you'll find that one of the perpetual dilemmas is how best to straddle the fine line between saying too much and saying too little. Do you try to justify your invitation to the story conference by gabbling out all your great ideas for enhancing the show before the morning coffee arrives, or venture so little that you risk coming across as the clutz most likely to contribute nothing?

What any sensible writer would do is follow some elementary middle-management meeting strategies such as observing the dynamics of the group, noting who always manages to engage the boss's ear and how they do it. This same shrewd scribe would employ that other simple but effective tactic of always restricting themselves to an opinion or suggestion on a few select storyline elements – preferably ones they really do know or feel particularly strongly about – rather than feeling the need to say something, anything, about everything.

Or, there's just shouting a lot.

The bare-knuckle brand of conference may sound like mayhem, but there is a chance that what comes out of it carries conviction. A storyline that's mooted and then booted about the park will invariably emerge – if it manages to – all the stronger. A character motivation that's bandied from the heart and that can be made to stand up against the hell-and-high-water of some equally passionate opposition is bound to come out carrying more validity on screen.

At one menagerie of a meeting where feelings were running particularly high over a major storyline, debate turned into a débacle so fierce that one writer fainted and another had walked out by 11 o'clock – a.m. What did eventually surface from a scrum that went on for some several more sweaty hours was a powerful tale that proved hugely popular.

But sometimes, however good the story you're proposing and however brilliantly you present it, it will not spark any interest. In these cases it helps to remember just how huge and ongoing Soap's appetite for stories is. The story idea that your colleagues and the Producer swept so carelessly off the table may well be greeted as veritable manna from heaven the next time the team is famished for inspiration.

Been there, done that

But back to smooth ingress, whatever the temperature of the meeting … What can help a new writer to get their feet under the story conference table is, as per the earlier advice, being (or appearing to be via those compilation videos) a regular follower of the show. Bucketloads of embarrassment can be avoided by not swanning in with a suggested storyline whereby Desmond gets Dolores pregnant when there was a six-week run of episodes last year about Desmond having a vasectomy.

Having said that, not being too rigid a disciple can have its advantages in that the newcomer hasn't become hidebound by the show's conventions. Long-running characters may be stuck in some stale groove simply because existing writers have been taking for granted that that's how they are. A less familiar eye can sometimes glimpse the character's potential for taking a different tack. In the best of all possible worlds this doesn't mean an unconvincing leap out of character as much as the development of a newly recognised facet.

But having said *that*, it's better on the whole to have boned-up on the show so far, if it's only to stop you endlessly suggest-ing storylines that are greeted by a group groan of 'been there, done that, did that twice over back in the Nineties'.

Listen before you leap

Even for those who've never missed an episode and are up to full speed with what's happening on screen at the time they sit in on the story conference, it pays to listen before launching in. That's because storylining conferences can – and usually do – take place several months before the episodes under discussion are transmitted. In other words, what's currently on screen is way out-of-date in terms of where the storylining is up to. It's time-wasting and useless to be vaunting a surefire audience-grabber wherein Dolores has a sex-change when production have just finished filming the ep where Dolores drowns herself.

Sometimes, when a new writer gets invited to the conference, the Script Editor will present them with a tottering stack of scripts that will bridge the gap between what's presently on screen and where the story conference is up to. When they don't there's no harm – and probably a couple of Brownie Points – in rookie writers asking to take a look at them. Should this seemingly conscientious request provoke a cagey response, it needn't be taken too personally. Mistrust, where it exists among script editors and producers, is general. Well, you never know, this new writer may only be posing as a new writer in order to get their hands on pre-production scripts so that they can run off and flog all the upcoming plots to a rival soap/the tabloids/teenage soapheads... Not that paranoia is rife in the Soap Opera world, you understand.

In the event of signing the Unofficial Secrets Act not being enough, the only solution is keeping a low profile in terms of suggesting any storylines until there's time to quiz the other writers over a pint or three. Hell, I know, but you have to do it.

Pre-meeting preparation

Once it's clear where the team are up to with their storytelling, a writer is expected – since to a greater or lesser degree, part of what they are being paid for is ideas – to put some serious thought into where the stories should be going next. Based on painful experience I can recommend that this were best done beforehand. A frantic brainstorming session with myself on the way into the car-park produced many a spark of pure genius. Until, of course, I got in there and delivered my brainchild with suitably modest aplomb – only to have it humiliatingly shot down from all sides before it could toddle.

Selling your idea: the three Bs

There's an old saying that there is only one most beautiful baby in the world – and every mother has it. By the same token, one's own ideas are bound to be one's favourites. When, as in the collaborative world of Soap, it comes to having to persuade your captains and colleagues to take your invention seriously, the idea needs to be Bullet, Bully and, moreover, Budget proof to stand a chance of being elected. Or, perhaps, *selected* would be a better word, as what you are trying to sell to the team is a story basis upon which all of you can build. The whole point of engaging your fellow writers in your core story idea is to elicit their input. It doesn't matter if the strand of your idea ends up taking different twists and turns from those you'd originally envisaged; your aim and the group goal is not anyone's story in particular, but the *best* story.

Bullet proof

Few Soap stories are completely self-contained, so the first thing to remember is that your suggested story idea has to work from all angles, including the spin-off effects it will inevitably have on other characters. Since your story is unlikely to be contained within a single episode, it helps to be able to tell it well enough to sell it to the other writers who, at some stage, are going to have to pick it up and run with it. It can be useful if, when you are struck by your wonderful storyline idea, you take the time and trouble to extrapolate from it and explore any long-term repercussions it may have.

A very simple device for convincing yourself of the depth and breadth of an idea before you throw it onto the story-conference table is to make yourself a rough chart. This can be as simple as listing all the major character names across the top of a page, marking the prime event under the title of the character it happens to, and then jotting down in the other characters' columns any consequences or effects your story idea may have on them. Another way to explore how far-reaching the effects of any one story idea might be is to take the core idea as the central planet and satellite off from it to surrounding characters. Yet another way of testing how much mileage your idea might have is to create a chart along the lines of a family tree: taking the core story idea and the character(s) most closely involved as the progenitor, draw downwards to the consequences on the next most closely affected character(s), and so on until you have enough to prove, at least to yourself, that there is plenty of spin-off substance to the idea.

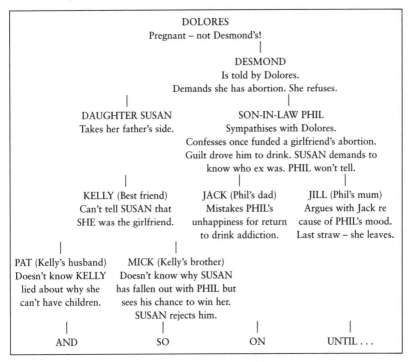

DOLORES
Pregnant – not Desmond's!

DESMOND
Is told by Dolores.
Demands she has abortion. She refuses.

DAUGHTER SUSAN
Takes her father's side.

SON-IN-LAW PHIL
Sympathises with Dolores.
Confesses once funded a girlfriend's abortion.
Guilt drove him to drink. SUSAN demands to
know who ex was. PHIL won't tell.

KELLY (Best friend)
Can't tell SUSAN that
SHE was the girlfriend.

JACK (Phil's dad)
Mistakes PHIL's
unhappiness for return
to drink addiction.

JILL (Phil's mum)
Argues with Jack re
cause of PHIL's mood.
Last straw – she leaves.

PAT (Kelly's husband)
Doesn't know KELLY
lied about why she
can't have children.

MICK (Kelly's brother)
Doesn't know why SUSAN
has fallen out with PHIL but
sees his chance to win her.
SUSAN rejects him.

AND   SO   ON   UNTIL . . .

. . . you have enough to show how useful and ongoing a catalyst your core story could be.

Of course, all the pre-meeting prep in the world won't guarantee that much or indeed any of your idea will be adopted, but your offering will at least provide a considered jumping-off point for the team to explore – for which they will be truly grateful if it's one of those grey days when there seems to have been an outbreak of brain-death that's left everyone stumped for suggestions.

Where the central idea does get taken on, but ramifications get altered during the course of discussion, the chart you made can also be used to help the group foresee the consequences of any such alterations. To demonstrate with a simple exercise, go back to son-in-law Phil's first appearance on the family tree.

Instead of him refusing to tell Susan who the ex-girlfriend was, have him forced into a confession that it was Susan's best friend Kelly. If Susan and Kelly are estranged it could help throw Susan into Mick's arms. There could also be a threat that Susan will reveal all to Kelly's husband.

The chart method may seem overly painstaking (and I'm not for a second suggesting that you should take it as far as appearing at the story conference with reams of spreadsheets), but at the dawn of an idea it can be easier than trying to hold the core story along with the whole scheme of knock-on effects in your head. Used as a personal initial tool it will allow you to examine the relative merits of various consequences for yourself and, when it comes to the story conference, can help you to put the case for the direction you think provides the richest storyline seam. On a more basic level, the chart will help to ensure that you haven't forgotten any of the major characters and/or the repercussions on them from any given storyline. This amnesia may seem unlikely – but on a Soap with a large list of major and regular peripheral characters it has been known. Many a meeting has found itself caught short with ten minutes to go by someone suddenly remembering that, in the process of juggling the fates and fortunes of so many, one character who would undoubtedly be affected has been left out of the equation.

What you do not want to take along to the meeting is so much detail and overly schematised mapping that your fellow writers will want to club up to take out a contract on you. What, ideally, you do want to go armed with is conviction and enough memory-jogging notes to show you've devoted some time to what you are asking your fellow team-members to consider.

Bully proof

To create balance, an astute producer will have picked team-members who are different but, hopefully, complementary. This inevitably means that there are those whose natures are more forceful than others. If your story idea is well prepared, you won't feel the need to enter into a slanging match with anyone trying to shout rather than argue your idea down. Having stated your well-thought-out case, you can afford to give your forceful colleague the floor and let the Producer decide if they have a story that's built on firmer ground than yours.

Budget proof

Each show has its budget limitations (*see* also Chapter 3). Your proposed idea needs to have taken account of it.

Pitching for a commission

In the case of the Soaps that hand out commissions on the basis of a writer's showing at the story conference, that can be a whole different can of worms – and you must learn to swallow this along with any overweening modesty you may have. To have to vie for commissions on the day – although they probably won't actually be offered on the day, but later by phone or via your agent – may not be seemly, but it can feel a damn sight more seemly than staying above it all and broke.

Even for those without stratospheric scruples or independent means, a first encounter with having to pitch for commissions can be tough. It's easy to be intimidated by the apparently endless knowledge, boundless life experience and seemingly bottomless passion of the other writers when it comes to the topics and character profiles that come up for discussion. Until, that is, you remember these people do fiction for a living.

I have seen (oh, all right, have been) a commission-hungry writer claiming not only to know but to care more deeply than most about (sensitive dispositions look away) ... quantity surveying. I know, I know. But faced with brazen competition there can seem little left but to pull some fictitious expertise and/or abiding fascination of your own out of thin air. Of course, as with any bluff, it only works if you can carry it off. Knowing what I later learned the hard way, I thank God I didn't sell myself into that particular one. Talking yourself into a deeply boring storyline or tedious character occupation means consigning yourself and your colleagues to trying to breathe some life into it for weeks, months and sometimes years to come.

Christmas comes but twice a year

When considering ideas to put to the team, the Soap writer needs to remember that the meeting will have been convened to plan episodes which will not be transmitted for some time – anything between two and six months, depending on the show.

(*See* also Chapter 3, pp. 37–8.) What this means is that when you are formulating your suggested storyline, it has to be set against the programme's production calendar rather than the real-life one. A meeting held at the back-end of July might well be planning the Christmas episodes, and although for the Scrooges among us the 'festering season' comes around quite often enough, you will have to put on your paper hat and get stuck into the Yuletide ideas. In my experience the silly-hat-wearing was only once not just metaphorical. In this mercifully rare instance of misguided think-tank management, the hapless writing team were literally issued with crêpe thinking-caps – along with crackers, balloons and blowers – and force-fed on mince pies in an effort to get us into the mood. I seem to remember it was a spirit we were somewhat slow to enter into. Understandable, perhaps, since any 'spirit' *was* strictly meta-phorical and, what's more, we were all inside while outside the only July sun any of us had seen was busy cracking the flags.

Incidentally (to this section on planning), the actual writing of these generally commemorated fests so far in advance can be an odd experience. I have found myself suddenly seized mid-script in January (my time) by a panic that I've forgotton to buy the kids' Easter eggs.

Going back to the planning stage, the motto is: Think Ahead. In run-of-the-mill terms this means not suggesting school stories that will be on screen during the long summer holidays, or family holiday stories when there would have to be an explanation as to why the kids aren't in school, and so on. One of the ways in which most home-grown Soaps hitch themselves to the audience's reality is to have their characters celebrating major calendar events in tandem, thus creating a commonality of preoccupations and experience. On some shows the writers are given a written or verbal note of events (as they will be occuring at transmission time) at the planning stage to stimulate appropriate ideas. And it is not just the most significant occasions – Christmas, New Year, royal weddings – that spawn the biggest stories. Valentine's Day, Hallowe'en, Mother's Day and the like can be the catalyst that sets characters on a new, long-running storyline stream, or impacts on already up-and-running themes. If, for instance, a character is already in financial difficulty, lonely or bored, an otherwise fairly commonplace annual event like the Grand National could be the genesis of anything from a gambling addiction to an extra-marital affair with someone they encountered at the betting shop. Where there is an already up-and-running storyline of, say, an elderly character's increasing mental instability, an event like Remembrance Sunday could have a cathartic effect.

Since these ordinary events can be such a rich seam, the writer does well to check for themselves or take account of the calendar when formulating storyline ideas – in other words to remember that, where Soap is concerned, Big Consequences from little Bank Holidays do grow.

Not talking yourself out of the job

Just how hard to defend your own precious plotline is another fine judgement. Soaps being a collaborative effort, you often have to give way to someone else's idea, and sensing just where to stop flogging your own favoured horse and start clambering graciously aboard a colleague's can be tricky. However, not timing it right can be costly. Arguing too long and too hard against an idea can end up precluding you, in the Producer's eyes, from writing it.

The facility for being seamlessly schizoid is, I suppose, as useful a skill as any for the Soap writer, since they need to be able to go home and write someone else's storyline with as much passion and commitment as they brought to trying to shout it down. If this seems at odds with the earlier impassioned rant about the best drama coming from writers who believe in what they are writing, it isn't. In Soap, writers have to be at one and the same time creative individuals and team players. On the face of it, a mutually exclusive state of affairs – but not when it's seen as a wholly proper combined effort which, within it, calls for each writer to do what he or she should do best: tell a truth. Not necessarily their own truth, but *a* truth from any and every character's perspective.

Getting picked to write the plums

You probably won't be offered a commission of any sort on the strength of one showing at a story conference. Some producers like you to attend several meetings before trusting you with a script. This is so you can get up to speed with where storylining is at, and so the Producer can get a sense of where your individual strengths or weaknesses might lie when it comes to executing any particular type of storyline.

On your first visit, the rest of the team can at least feel secure in mind and pocket knowing that newcomers rarely, if ever, get handed plum episodes on a first outing. Not that, I must hasten to add, all competition for commissions is to do with filthy old lucre. A proportion of it has as much to do with kudos as cash. How many episodes a writer is asked to do, and, as crucially, how many *big* ones – in the sense of headline-grabbing births, marriages, murders, and almost anything homosexual – is seen as denoting a writer's standing within the group.

It's cloud cuckoo time expecting to walk in and get The One Where Desmond Finally Snaps. A lot of money, time and effort will be spent on publicising it – or surreptitiously leaking it to the press – and there's little to no chance of the Producer trusting a writer with it until they've proved themselves competent on some of the less pivotal episodes. If the commission up for grabs is for an episode that's going foreign, the last writer in can almost certainly forget about getting it. When The Powers-That-Be have decided to invest in Desmond and Dolores visiting any location from Benidorm to Burundi, the competition for what will most likely be a complementary familiarisation trip for the writer will be fierce – to say the least.

Conscience versus commission

On any Soap there will inevitably be those times when the writer doesn't like what they're being asked to write. And I have to say that, in my experience, this tends to happen less when shows are writer-led. Where creative democracy doesn't exist, or has been abandoned in favour of the handing-down of tablets-of-stone storylines, the question of writers' integrity has a tendency to pop up more often. This is especially true where producers don't see the need for writers to necessarily believe what they write – and truer still when producers make it clear that the show's only ethic is ratings.

The concept that many writers find it hardest to reconcile themselves to is one that seldom falls from fellow writers' lips, but tumbles all too often out of the mouths of producers: 'They won't understand it.' 'They' being the audience and 'it' being everything from a word with more than six letters to a motivation with seven. Ask the Producer if they mean that they themselves don't understand it, and they look downright insulted. Are they implying that someone else in the room doesn't know what it means? Perish the thought. What they do know is that outside their window the comprehension quotient drops to something just above brain-death.

Of course, those writers who are outraged on the audience's behalf can always challenge the logic of this piece of gross patronage. Isn't the very fact that Soap sets out to reflect life back to its audience recognition that that audience is actually out there living it? And if this same audience is out there doing it for real, dealing every day with issues more difficult and complicated than any drama could devise, do they really need those lives reflecting back to them in words of one syllable? Where this counter-argument consistently falls on stony ground, there is only one of two ways for the writer to go – out the door or home to write the best they can around a construct of contempt.

Whether working on a writer-led show or not, few Soap writers can claim to have put conscience over commission all of the time – and I'm not one of them. There have been too many meetings when I've sat through, or added my twopenneth to, the formulation of storylines that were frankly rank with cynicism. Conversely, I have at times counted myself among writers fighting tooth-and-nail for the right to create something honourable. I know which work I've felt proudest of but, in the end, each writer has to decide for themselves just how much compromise is too much.

And, of course, we all have our different sticking points. Even the take-the-money-and-run writers sometimes surprise themselves by finding they've stumbled up against a plot or character point they simply can't stomach. Watching a misanthrope turn martyr over a credibility gap too far is fascinating. Watching them lose the argument underlines one of the central dilemmas of Soap writing: it's someone else's naff story/character-leap, so it will serve them right if they fall flat on their face writing it. On the other hand, since you're a part of the communal soul they are bent on selling out, would it be better to lend the nonsense some credence by making sure it at least gets written well? Which means, of course, by you.

Sometimes it's not a question of feeling that you'd be morally 'selling out' to write a particular storyline. The disinclination to write someone else's idea may be because it seems to you to be inconsequential, not your particular cup of tea, or just downright boring. Decide to take it on, though, and writing under such circumstances can prove interesting. Left to our own devices, writing about what we instinctively know, love and find fascinating is what most of us choose to do. But having to drum up passion and perception offers the opportunity for a more objective exploration. Not hamstrung by seeing the storyline from any particular standpoint, the writer landed with someone else's baby can sometimes make a better job of raising it. They may well see angles that the original instigator of the idea could not – and, in an effort to counter their own boredom with some storyline topic, may dig all the deeper and actually find some fascinating facet.

Favourites are for fans

The audience can have darlings, but the Producer needs ideas for everyone in the Soap's cast. As a writer you may not like the character you are writing; you may not espouse their values, admire their goals, their tactics or their motives; but you do have to make them 'real'. Of course it's tempting to concentrate on your favourites – the more likeable, colourful or laudable – but neglecting the rest usually turns out to be a snare and a delusion.

Drama, whatever the genre, relies heavily on conflict of one sort or another, be it the inner sort surrounding love, hate or jealousy, the conflict of interest in work and relationships, or the flying-sparks variety made from rubbing two conflicting personalities together. And you can't have convincing conflict with or within a cardboard cutout. Even your beloved, best-drawn characters will end up looking exposed when sooner or later they come up against a flimsier figment of the writer's imagination. Without an opponent of equal weight, the best actor in the world can't help but look as if they're just shadow-boxing.

I suppose one of the differences between the Soap writer and the solitary scribe is that the latter gets to choose each and every character they strive to bring to life, whereas the Soap writer often has to weave texture into creatures not of their own making. Call it schizoid, call it being flexible, call it, if you must, cupidity – I call it a considerable skill.

You'll have gathered by now that I believe any story conference worth the having will spend almost as much time debating who the characters are as it does what they're going to do. Showing some insight and interest in character make-up and motivation should – if there's any sense and fairness knocking around – move the writer a step closer to that coveted commission.

Long-term storylining

As touched upon earlier when discussing the writer's remit, you may be asked to attend long-term planning sessions in addition to the regular storyline meetings. Again, depending on how the show is organised, these meetings can either involve the handing-down of edicts from On High or be a genuinely open debate between the Producer and writers about what issues and stories should be tackled and what characters should come, stay or go.

Long-term planning is a great idea overall, even though some portion of it will invariably end up going awry for one reason or another. New characters can be devised down to the colour of their eyes and what newspaper they read, and be cast with every bit as much attention and aforethought, but it will not necessarily make the audience take to them. This means that they may have to be written out again, taking the storyline they were designed to carry along with them. By the same token, characters planned to be of only minor significance can become huge in the audience's affections overnight. And where a peripheral character becomes unexpectedly popular, the scheme of things will need shifting to put them more in the limelight.

Story strands themselves can beggar the best-laid plans. What was predicted to be compulsive may have the viewers turning off in droves. Just as a supposed brief encounter can, by popular demand, need turning into a long-running affair.

Why some characters don't work

In the case of a particular character, the audience's reasons for attraction or otherwise is, in the end, in the same realms as the litmus reactions we have to anyone in real life. A matter of mysterious chemistry which my Dad used to sum up with philosophical flatness as: 'Nice fella – nobody likes him.'

Why some storylines don't work

Whether storylines sink or swim is sometimes a more quantifiable case of timing. Writers, having an overdeveloped ear for life as it goes on around them, very often have the other ear to the ground when it comes to upcoming swings in society. Almost spookily often they will tap into a change of attitude or public perception while it is still nought but a glimmer in the group consciousness. This is a useful facility when it comes to second-guessing what topics, issues and social mores will be in vogue when storylines that have to be formulated months beforehand finally hit the screen – but it is by no means an infallible one.

Topicality works a treat

Failing to coincide what's on screen with what's on the audience's mind by as little as a month or so either way can sign a story's death warrant. Too soon, and it's of minority interest; too late and it's old hat. When the inexact science of creative precognition does conspire with Fate to put an issue on screen at the same time as a national groundswell of opinion or interest, it's not only gratifying for the writers but, for the audience, adds to the illusion that the evening's episode must have been written that very morning. This appearing to be topical is the difference between expecting viewers to enter a pre-packaged construct of reality and seeming to enter theirs. In the suspension-of-disbelief business the second is always more satisfying all round.

The show's the thing

There is another way in which long-term planning can turn out to be something of a snare and a delusion, and that is in the risk of storylines becoming set in concrete. An overall arc defining the general direction in which everyone involved sees the show going is fine, as is trying to make sure that characters do not get tramlined in the wrong direction. But if, as the storylines unfold across the weeks and months, different and better ideas emerge, the writers or storyliners need to be able to step outside the master plan they devised for themselves at the long-term planning stage. It's non-productive for any team-member to sulk or shout that a diversion isn't on simply because it deviates from what was agreed. The Soap professional's only question should be: 'Is it better for the show?'

3. Whey-hey! A Commission! Now What?

So here we are. The writer's sat through several story conferences at which they've shone with quiet intelligence, shown a sound knowledge of past storylines, laughed not too ingratiatingly at the Producer's jokes, not snaffled all the best biscuits, ventured some modest but interesting ideas and not got too far up the noses of the rest of the writing team. The reward for this model behaviour is finally to be given the chance to write an episode.

A first outing will probably be described as 'a trial', but it will almost certainly be a mistake to assume that this means being allowed an infinite number of shots at getting it right. Soap 'virgins' are usually granted some margin of error; however, the very fast turn-around schedule of maintaining production on weekly drama means that no-one will have time to nurse people endlessly through the writing process.

One of the things the Producer has to be confident about, apart from an ability to write well, is a talent for doing it as quickly as the schedule requires. Whether the writing time you have been allotted is a couple of weeks or a couple of months, you will have been provided from the outset with a delivery date for your script or scripts. You may even have been given a specific time on a specific day (before 10.30 a.m. or whatever) as the point at which your commission must be on someone's desk.

You can ask for all the help you like (and you'll most likely get it) between commission and deadline, but if you fail to make the finishing post on time the overwhelming odds are in favour of you not getting offered another commission. If you are floundering so hopelessly halfway through the writing that you have to admit to not being able to complete the script on time, it is entirely likely that you will be paid off and another writer commissioned to do a hasty job on your episode. This situation – where an episode has to be picked up by another writer – can also happen to regular, experienced team-members. When, by way of some genuine incapacity or tragedy, a writer is prevented from working, another writer has to be given the job of finishing the script by the allotted time. It stands to reason that no episode can be left out of the ongoing chain, so *an* episode must be produced – no matter who ends up writing it.

If you haven't already gathered , the upshot of all this is that, where Soap is concerned, deadlines are not negotiable.

What's the hurry?

It sometimes seems extraordinary to newcomers that the script they are writing has to be produced in such an unholy rush when it is not scheduled to appear on screen for up to several months. This apparently long time 'twixt script and screen shrinks to something even more extraordinary when you realise what has to happen to that script as it moves through its various production stages.

To name but a dozen, each and every episode involves:

- The nomination and booking of a Director.
- An unsung Admin Department to process, duplicate and distribute production copies of the scripts both to the cast members and multifarious department staff, including –
- Wardrobe Department, who will need to assess costume requirements in order to find or acquire what's appropriate.
- Make-Up, who need notice of how many cast-members will require their services for standard and/or special (e.g. accident) make-up.
- Casting Department to schedule regular actors for read-throughs, rehearsals and the actual shoot, as well as finding, auditioning and booking non-regular characters and any extras required.
- Design Department, who need notice of what set-dressing is required for the various scenes. Most long-running Soaps have a number of the most frequently used sets permanently mounted, but these still need arranging according to individual scenes. (That pile of washing in back of shot doesn't get there on its own.) Inevitably, there will also be requirements from time to time for non-standard sets such as hospital

waiting rooms, a headteacher's office, etc. Shows with a more generous budget can afford to shoot these in some actual location, but since most try to be as cost-effective as they can, the designer often ends up having to dress somewhere on-site to fit the bill. It's one of the minor miracles of television that a corner of the staff canteen can between breakfast and lunch turn into what will look on screen like a five-star restaurant or that, in the twinkle of a designer's skill, the finance office turns into a hospital delivery suite.

- As far as on-site exterior scenes go, these can also involve the gardener and/or groundsman if, for instance, a scene actually shot in August is going to call for a character to be ankle-deep in autumn leaves.
- Lighting Department to plan requirements for each and every scene. All scenes will need to be lit. Moreover, any interior scene purporting to be taking place at night but actually scheduled to be shot during the daytime may call for blackout curtains, and exterior night shoots require special lighting.
- Camera Department, so that they can plan equipment requirements and camera angles, particularly anything complicated involving cranes, etc.
- Sound Department, who need to organise for those precious words to get heard whatever the background.
- Continuity, who need notice of being on-hand to make sure, for example, that contiguous scenes which are not, for logistical reasons, shot continuously look the same as far as both set and actors are concerned.
- Research/Researcher – *see* Chapter 9.

All this and more – and that's without even mentioning the editing and dubbing processes – to bring one single script to the screen alongside what could be some 150-odd other episodes a year for a show that goes out three times a week. Which goes some way to explaining why there'll be limited time to bring a new writer up to speed.

Courage, mon ami!

That said, the first-timer can't afford to become paralysed by how much rests on them getting it right. Enough panic to produce the required adrenalin is, however, useful. To stop you feeling too exposed, producers often have the sense to cushion newness between episodes written by more experienced hands, and old soldiers on either side are usually pretty good about giving novices the benefit of their wisdom.

To give the inexperienced an even better fighting chance, it's unlikely that they will have been given more than a single episode to write on their first outing. Veteran crew-members will have worked their way up to writing three or more episodes in the time the newcomer will have available to produce just one – but it's as well for the novice not to get used to such luxury, as success with a single episode will soon breed into the expectation that the writer can manage more.

Firming up the brief

Again, Soaps do vary in the way these things are structured, but there will probably be some form of meeting after the commission is offered and before the writer is expected to begin. If not a meeting, then there will be a lengthy phone call from an editor or producer. Prior to this meeting (or phone call) the writer will most likely have been sent a breakdown of all the episodes in that writing block, including the episode(s) they have been commissioned to write. This is another element of the job that racks up non-writing time, since the writer needs to study not only their own episode breakdown, but its relation to the rest of the set.

When what the writer has been invited to is a full commissioning meeting, it will involve the several other writers who have been asked to produce episodes in that particular block. This will obviously go quicker and more smoothly if everyone has done their preparation thoroughly, since the purpose of this get-together is to make sure that each individual writer is clear about what storyline strands take place in their particular episode(s), as well as to help iron out the potential cross-over points between scripts.

Avoiding cross-over

For instance, an episode may call for Dolores and Desmond to be arguing. If it is a one-off row designed to be contained in a single episode, the writer obviously has no problem other than to write it convincingly. If, however, the row started to rumble in a previous episode and is ongoing throughout the next one or several, the writer needs to come to some understanding with the writers on either side about who covers what elements.

In A's episode, the row may be in its infantile stage of sulks and slammed doors. In B's, Dolores may be attempting to bring the grievance out into the open, while Desmond does his utmost to sideline the problem. In C's episode, Dolores may be beginning to despair of Desmond's ability to confront the problem. If the inevitable showdown is not scheduled to happen until D's episode, it's obvious that there is endless potential for writers A, B and C to repeat each other in terms of the way in which the two characters demonstrate their emotions. Refining the broad plot to the degrees of anger, despondency, despair, etc., and deciding how best to vary their manifestation throughout the run of episodes, doesn't guarantee that writers won't end up overlapping and echoing each other to some extent – but it will certainly reduce the possibility.

It also makes sense at the commissioning-meeting stage to clear up any points in an episode breakdown which are open to misinterpretation. If, for example, a breakdown says, 'It is obvious that Dolores is attracted to him,' it saves time and trouble down the line to ask your Producer just *how* obvious he or she envisages this attraction being. Barely perceptible to slight? Slight to moderate? Or moderate to overt? If the episode breakdown doesn't cover it, it's as well to check whether the character's attraction ought to be perceptible only to the audience, or whether the recipient should notice it, or if it is to be noticed by other character(s).

The wages of not doing this pre-meeting prep and turning up primed with such questions will inevitably be getting stuck during the precious writing time. Choices then are having to ring to ask for the clarification that should rightly have been sought earlier, or to risk winging it with a guess about what the Producer must have meant.

The perils are that uncertainty tends to show up in the writing and/or the guess will prove to be resoundingly wrong. In other words, tardiness at the start stands every chance of ending up as a self-inflicted rewrite – and, believe me, no writer wants to add to the weight of those.

Oi! That was *my* storyline!

No amount of preparation will protect the writer from the odd time when an unscrupulous colleague decides they like your storyline better than than their own and proceeds to nick it from under your nose. There's no way of knowing your goodies have been hijacked until you receive the first drafts of all the episodes in the block.

Fairness won't come into it when you claim that they, not you, should have to erase the storyline now duplicated in two scripts. The Producer will simply choose the version he or she likes best and, if it isn't yours, you'll be doing the rewrite.

Time to stop talking

On the whole, if the writer was punctilious before and at the commissioning meeting, they are in a much more comfortable position when it comes to sitting down to start the actual writing.

And it's as well to *be* comfortable as, given the deadline, there isn't much leeway for moving around much until the job's done. The washing just has to pile to Eiger proportions; the kids have to sort out their own squabbles and sports kit; partners, PMT, friends, lovers, pastimes and life in general just have to stay on the back-burner until those three magic words 'End of Episode' are thunked thankfully out.

But where to start?

For there to be an ending, of course, there has to be a start. Given the careful planning that went on at the story conference and later at the commissioning stage you might, at about this point, be thinking that this, surely, is where Soap writing has something of a head start.

Day One will see the scriptwriter, as in other forms of creative writing, confronted with the proverbial blank page – or nagging cursor – but at least in Soap it's a slightly simpler case of how to begin, not where. True. But only up to a point. Where one episode starts is, obviously, where it has been decided that the last episode will leave off. That point, which is known as 'The Cliff' or 'The Hook', will have been an all-important issue at the story conference – or specified by the storyliner(s) – so you'll be well aware of what it is. The Soap writer's first dilemma is to find a way of picking it up. And hooks must always be picked up (*see* also Chapter 7).

Structuring your work

Working to a given structure

Where the writer has been provided with an already structured and very detailed scene breakdown for their episode, how they pick up the hook and run with it will already have been decided. In this case the writer can set about the job of inventing believable dialogue and bringing life to the bare bones of their story outline.

Creating your own structure

When, however, it's a case of working for shows that expect the writer to create their own episode structure, there's obviously some more work to be done before starting to write the episode. How much time is spent on up-front planning is down to the individual. Some writers can't begin the actual writing process until they have carefully plotted every scene in detail. Others do no pre-planning at all, trusting to luck and instinct when it comes to making their quart fit into its pint pot.

The route map

A third way to approach the writing is to create a roughly sketched scene breakdown – a route map which satisfies the writer that they'll have time to call at all the spots of special interest, while leaving them some room for manoeuvre in between.

The starting point will have to take account of the pick-up of the previous episode's hook, while the destination will be the predetermined hook of the episode in hand. The writer will invariably have some sort of storyline breakdown to work from, so it is a relatively simple matter to scan this for the most crucial plot elements and emotional highs and lows and jot them down against a list of scene numbers. As it's also important to keep in mind the logistics of placing the required action against the background of a limited number of sets and locations, this route-map method can also help to determine the overall episode plan.

However you get there – get there on time

The rough route map may seem on the face of it to be the most sensible approach. Too rigid a plan, and the writer can find themselves hopelessly hung by their own tightly woven noose; while no plan at all can lead to an equally serious panic-attack when, three-quarters way through the script, there dawns the awful realisation that so far, none of the major plot points have been dealt with.

I qualify the middle way as seeming sensible 'on the face of it' because, in the end, writing is more a thing of temperament than time-and-motion. Where method is concerned there is only what works for the person doing it. A writer can be as aware as all-fall-down of the pitfalls of tramlining themselves with a tight structure, or of leaving themselves swinging in the wind with only two hours' writing time left, but it won't make a jot of difference to the way they find they can work. Start the minute they get home from the commissioning conference or alternatively spend the first two-thirds of the writing allocation shampooing the carpets, the curtains and the cat: it makes no odds and it's no skin off the Script Editor's nose – as long as the job gets done. On time.

No muse is good muse

This *carte blanche* in how a writer gets to the finishing line isn't the same as saying that Soap producers can afford to indulge free-spirited, creative concepts like inspiration. The process simply can't hang around waiting for the Muse to strike, so the Producer has to see the commission he or she hands out as all the inspiration anyone should need.

That's why you will rarely hear among a rabble of Soap Opera writers any mention of Writer's Block. When two or three are gathered together they may well be petitioning for bigger bucks, smaller agents' fees, and a word-processor package they can cajole into numbering the pages, but talk of needing a literary laxative to get them going – now that really would be naïve.

Restrictions on the writer

Considering the cost

However prescriptive or not the actual scene breakdown, there will be other restrictions to consider when planning the writing of an episode. These are not to do with characterisation or content but purely, simply and crucially to do with cost.

Although it involves creativity and artistry of many kinds, Soap is a product every bit as real as the sort sitting on the wash-basin. Where a channel produces its own Soap, it expects it to be manufactured – as with all its other programmes – within a strict budget. Where a channel buys in a ready-made show it will only be prepared to pay so much and no more for it. Whoever dictates the budget, it is finite. It needs to be, since nothing, apart from film, can run away with money faster than television. You only have to look at the credits at the end of any show to realise that the personnel list runs on further than I've mentioned so far. Even then, these are only the tip of the iceberg. Behind those named as appearing are those employed to publicise the fact. There are drivers and people who clap clapperboards. There is also a vital artisan workforce, and surrounding the whole is another small army employed to feed, clean and keep secure the entire shebang.

Every scene, no matter how short, carries the hidden cost of this multitude on its back. That's why the writer will find that there is a tacit or strictly stipulated quota for how many scenes there can be in any one episode.

Scene allowance

As was mentioned earlier, every venue that a writer specifies as a background to the action – be it a room, corridor, garden, street, office or whatever – has to be rigged for lighting, sound and camera . . . each time it is used. Two separate scenes within one episode may have been written to take place in the same sitting room, but they can't be counted as one scene in production-cost terms because they may not be shot on the same day. Yes, it would seem sensible if they were, but life on Planet Telly just isn't like that.

Just as three minutes of script does not equate to three minutes of the writer's time, the process of getting that three minutes on camera translates into many hours by the time the set's dressed, rigged for light and sound and the actors have performed to the Director's satisfaction.

It's no use either the writer trying to get around a restriction on scene numbers by pretending that continuous action counts as one. It doesn't. Many have tried and all, including me, have failed to convince the Producer that action opening on Dolores in the bedroom which then follows her into the bathroom, downstairs, through the hallway and out into the garden (via the kitchen) is one scene.

It's six. Seven if the Producer's going to nit-pick about the upstairs landing. But, either way, if you're working to a brief of only 15–18 scenes per episode it's still about five too many. With a host of other characters and several more storylines to carry in what's left of the scene allocation, a writer can find themselves hopelessly caught short and resorting towards the end to improbable mass gatherings.

Fancy seeing you here!
Even where the allocation is more generous – say up to 20-odd scenes – fitting everything and everybody in is still a logistical challenge, not to say nightmare. On average there'll be two or three major and at least two minor storylines jostling for a place in the scheme of things. Since this is Soap, where all elements are ongoing and unalterable without massive repercussions, there can be no leaving anything out. It's up to the writer to engineer plausible overlaps of characters coming and going against the backdrop of one scene – and it's where, if you didn't, you can wish you'd done that bit of up-front planning.

Obviously, if the Soap has a regular social venue such as a local pub, shop or café, such overlaps are relatively simple to devise. But even then it has to seem natural that the characters involved would coincide in that particular place at that particular time of day or night.

Locations
A further restriction will undoubtedly be the number of locations which a writer is allowed to use in any one episode. The difference between a set and a location is that the location costs *a lot* more. The huge expense of dressing and rigging a set on a show's own campus is as nothing compared to taking the actors

and crew out into the real world. The location will invariably have to be paid for. Whatever anyone tells you, TV crews leave a mess (hence the payment of a facility fee to whoever lends them the venue) and can damage your church, courtroom, floral gardens or whatever to a degree that calls for the provision of insurance cover.

Transport is needed to get everyone to the location and, once there, everyone will demand some form of catering – even if it's only a double de-caff and a bun.

Once the gaffer's risked life and limb stringing cables from every pillar and post, the sound man's had a little weep over the worst acoustics he's ever come across, the Director's thrown his morning strop, and the shoot is finally underway, it is relatively easy to exercise some control over an interior location. That is, until you're halfway through a tearjerker of a wedding scene and the verger/builder/lady-who-always-does-the-flowers-on-a-Tuesday turns up because no-one told *them* they were filming that silly Soap-thing – which, incidentally, they never watch.

Exterior locations are different. They are much worse.

Sod's Law of Soaps says that everything that can screw up a shoot will do so – big style. The only seagull in town will drop by to anoint any carefully coiffed character; jets will divert to drown out any crucial speech; double-deckers will decant St Trinianesque hordes; and drunks, derelicts and all manner of passers-by will materialise to stand grinning in the back of shot. Failing such visitations you can always rely on the weather to ruin everything.

The cast list

As well as being restricted in terms of scenes and locations, the Soap writer is likely to find themselves working under another ceiling when it comes to the number of actors they are allowed to use per episode.

The size of cast allocation will vary depending, obviously, on the show's budget, but once fixed it is usually no more elastic than the scene allowance. This isn't because actors get paid silly money for appearing in Soaps – most of them get surprisingly little for the stamina and versatility they turn in week after week – but because they do get paid something and whatever that is times 20-odd is a considerable wage bill.

Minor transitory characters can and sometimes do cost less – unless they're a star doing a guest appearance – but they still have to be taken account of in budgetary terms. And that means in the writer's terms too. Extras are cheaper again, but write more than several words for them to speak and they turn into a Part. And Parts get paid more than Non-Speaking Parts. It all adds up, which is why your Producer will want to keep the cast list down.

Actors also get – need – time off. In this case it isn't the stinginess of the budget that's to blame for them not being on your cast of available characters, but the fact that the actor may well have been scheduled to be taking a well-deserved rest when what's being written reaches the rehearsal and shoot stage.

Some of the major long-running characters in the higher profile television Soaps are given contracts that will guarantee them a specified number of episodes throughout a given period. (This can also apply to regular Soap writers but it is – lamentably – less common.) Such contract arrangements with actors assures them of regular work and income which, in turn, assures the programme-makers of their availability. It's a luxury that some of the lower-budget Soaps can't run to. Certainly in radio, where programmes are expected to be made at a fraction of the cost of television, this mutual security is seen as neither afford-able nor fair. Since a radio actor's fees are so relatively small, programme-makers don't consider it enough to demand their actor's exclusivity. On a show such as *The Archers*, actors aren't booked until the last minute: this allows them the flexibility to combine their radio work with more lucrative acting jobs. The benefit to the programme of this non-contractual policy is that the show retains the calibre of actor that it may not otherwise be able to afford. It does, however, mean that producers and writers can never be absolutely certain that the characters they want for any given episode will be available. It's a testimony to all concerned that what is frequently some hasty and *very* last-minute lateral juggling with plotlines because of actors' non-availability is rarely, if ever, evident in transmission.

Hamlet without the Prince
Even when actors' time off or non-availability has been taken into account well in advance, and some off-screen time planned for their character, their absence can pose problems for the writer.

Long-running characters will invariably be either significantly or peripherally involved in ongoing storylines that straddle their time off, and they will need to appear to be so. Devising ways of mentioning characters enough to make it feel as if they're around somewhere but not so much that it points up their absence, as well as keeping storylines simmering nicely even when they are on the back-burner, is a small yet vital art in itself.

As is keeping a character alive when it's the plot that calls for them to be 'away' for any length of time. Since out of sight is very soon out of the audience's mind for even the most popular of characters, some devices for regular mentions should properly be built in at the storylining stage. Should it get overlooked, it's up to the writer to notice that Desmond seems to have dropped off the face of the earth with last month's storyline to boot. Fail to, and it's odds-on that somebody else will clock it at some point down the line – usually just when you think you've finished the episode. Either way, it's often part of the Soap writer's lot to be constructing episodes without a central character, and it's one of the places where subtlety – or lack of it – can show up most.

So, there we have it. All the commissioned writer has to do is decide how they will juggle two or three current major storylines, a couple of minor ones plus a back-burner or two, using only a limited amount of scenes, locations and characters, into a 30-minute episode.

Time out

Except there aren't actually 30 minutes in a half-hour episode. Just as there aren't 15 minutes in a quarter-of-an-hour slot.

Above and beyond all other rationing there is time, and the terrible lack of it, for the writer of Soap to contend with. On average a half-hour television episode with no commercial break will, after opening and closing credits have been docked, leave the writer some 26 minutes in which to tell the multifarious tales of many. With a bite taken out for the ads the available space shrinks to something around 22 minutes. Not bad when you work out the writer's fee per minute. But not that easily earned when you consider that what the writer has to do in that short ration of moments is not only capture and keep an audience but build to a point that'll have them clamouring for more (*see* also pp. 6–12, *Notes for new writers*).

48

4. Page One, Scene One, Speech One

Armed either with a structured template provided by others or with their own route map, the writer can now set about the writing proper. Since, even for new writers, their involvement so far will almost certainly have given them access to fellow writers' scripts, it will be pretty clear that there are patterns to be followed when it comes to both format and writing style. This chapter will deal with many of those basic elements of script construction and dialogue creation, but bear in mind that the following three chapters also contain some Soap-specific elements that the writer needs to take into account.

But to begin at the beginning, a Soap script will need the following.

Scene headings

(Example)

<u>Sc. 01   INT.   DENTS' SITTING ROOM   DAY</u>

- Scenes are always numbered consecutively. Sometimes the writer is required to state the episode number as well as the scene number, e.g. Sc. 1740.01.
- INT. or EXT. is used to denote INTERIOR or EXTERIOR setting.
- Where the scene takes place (e.g. DENTS' SITTING ROOM) is always stipulated in the heading. Take care to describe the same setting in exactly the same manner each time it is used for subsequent scenes. If you suddenly change it to LIVING ROOM halfway through your script, the time-poor, panic-rich production team may read it as a different room and another set-up altogether.

- DAY or NIGHT. An indication of when the scene takes place is always necessary. This setting of time will be useful to the production team throughout the making of the episode. Even before then, at the pre-production stage, your indication of how much DAY or NIGHT shooting is required will help in assessing how affordable (or not) your episode is likely to be. All shoots, whether interior or exterior, will need lighting; but DAY shooting is relatively simple and inexpensive compared to NIGHT shooting. Interior NIGHT shooting may have to be done during the daytime which may involve blacking-out the set.

  Note: Exterior NIGHT is usually considered an expensive option and writers are often required to be sparing in their use of this setting.

- SPECIFIC TIMING. Instead of just stipulating DAY or NIGHT in a scene heading, the writer may be required to give a specific time (e.g. 3.45 p.m. or 15.45 or whenever). This requirement will vary from show to show. If you are submitting a script on spec and don't know the show's preference, it's probably wisest to stick to DAY or NIGHT, although it will make the pace of your episode seem more naturalistic if you keep a sense of the timing in your head. In other words, if you have Dolores leaving for an outing at the end of a scene, it will seem odd if you cut to the next scene and then cut back after 30 seconds to find Dolores returned. If you have in mind that Dolores left at one o'clock and that she would return at, say, two-thirty, you can judge the pace and content of the intervening scene or scenes to give a convincing impression of that amount of time having passed.

  Another way in which your time-setting for a scene will be useful is during the rehearsal and shooting stages. Where scenes are not shot in script sequence (which they often aren't), the time set on the heading will provide all concerned with a quick reference as to where they are in the scheme of things.

- For television scripts it is usual for each new scene to start on a new page; whereas with radio, a double line of spacing between the end of one scene and the heading for the next is usually sufficient.

General script notes

- Characters' names should always appear in CAPITAL LETTERS – unless, that is, the name appears in the dialogue. (DOLORES: I was going to ask Desmond if he wanted to come.) Whether or not the capitalised name is underlined (<u>DOLORES</u>:) varies according to in-house styles.
- Refer to characters in exactly the same way throughout the script. DOLORES shouldn't suddenly become MRS DENT or vice-versa, and neither should she nor any other character be reduced to mere initials.
- OOV is sometimes used as shorthand for Out of Vision. For an example of how this can be used, *see* the sample script on pp. 132–61.
- POV – shorthand for Point of View, when you would like something to be seen as from a particular character's standpoint (e.g. FROM RON'S POV).
- Other than this, the etiquette is usually that you do not stipulate too many specific camera angles: that is the Director's province (*see* also below).

Stage directions

These are not often covered in much detail in books about scriptwriting but, to my mind, they are crucial and are where the writer needs to demonstrate as much skill in composing prose as they do in producing dialogue. Before dealing with the different types of stage directions and what they are designed to do, a word about how the requirement for Soap stage directions can vary from what is generally acceptable for other sorts of scriptwriting.

In any writing for film or television there is always the knotty question of just how specific a writer ought to be when it comes to supplying stage directions. When writing scripts for Soap, finding the right balance can be particularly tricky. The usual sound advice when it comes to single drama (a play or a film) is that the writer should keep the use of stage directions down to a bare minimum. This protocol is recommended on the basis that, whereas it is the writer's job to create dialogue, the ultimate realisation of a scene falls more properly to the Director and actors. For the writer to stipulate how each speech ought to be delivered can (understandably) be interpreted as a slur on the creativity of directors and actors alike.

In Soap, though, writers are sometimes asked to be slightly more specific and fulsome in their use of stage directions. This is not because the actors and directors are any less skilled at interpreting the material, but is to do with the unusually fast pace of Soap production schedules. Since rehearsal time is very short for Soap actors and directors, it matters that the writer takes some care in providing them with clear and concise stage directions and mood notes.

You had to be there

The Soap scriptwriter has also to bear in mind that the Director and actors won't have been at the planning meetings and, there-fore, won't be as up-to-date with upcoming storylines as the writer will be. If, say, it is going to matter to the story later on in the series that Dolores looks shifty for what appears to be no obvious reason, it is up to the writer to make the directions in their script very clear indeed. And, as an added precaution, if it's one of the shows that affords the writer a meeting with the Director, it's as well to point out Dolores' seemingly unaccount-able behaviour to him or her as being important to a future storyline.

With the single play or short series, everyone involved in production has the luxury of much more time to concentrate on the nuances of the text and sub-text of every piece of dialogue. Given Soap's breakneck pace, it can be helpful then if the writer goes slightly further than normal when it comes to stipulating the intention of a speech or scene – thus saving time at the production stage. Which is not to say that the writer should provide lengthy and meticulously detailed wodges of direction. What is required is succinct description that creates a mental picture of what the characters are doing, seeing and feeling.

How and where the different types of stage directions should appear in a script – capital letters, underlining, etc. – varies from show to show as well as from television to radio. I've used a selection of programme styles in the following examples, which are primarily designed to illustrate the writing techniques rather than layout.

Five different directions

There are basically five main job categories when it comes to what stage directions are employed to do. The first comes directly beneath the scene heading and is sometimes known as a 'scene intro'.

SCENE INTROS

Throughout a script, each and every scene should start by describing the point at which we join this particular slice of story. In Soap writing, where the set is in regular use, there is no need to describe the geography of a room that is already familiar to the Director, actors and audience. Unless there is something out of the ordinary about the ordinary setting – for instance, ransacked following a robbery, more than normally tidy or untidy, mid-decorating job – the scene heading will suffice. Where all concerned know the Dents' kitchen almost as well as their own, we can go straight into an opening such as DOLORES IS DASHING TO AND FRO SETTING THE TABLE.

What *is* crucial is that the writer keep any established set firmly in mind as they write, so as to avoid wasting everyone's time by calling for logistical impossibilities. If, for instance, the Dents' sitting room contains only armchairs, Desmond can't come in and throw himself on the sofa, just as Dolores cannot swan in through French windows that aren't there. Since the audience knows that furniture and features don't just appear from nowhere in their own surroundings, unexplained alterations can't happen in Soap if it is to maintain any sense of reality.

In the famous case of *Brookside*'s body under the patio, the storyline was conceived at a point at which there *was* no patio. Aware of how familiar the audience was with the house's back garden, the writers had to set about devising a separate, credible and entertaining storyline which involved several other of the show's characters in the planning and laying of what would later become Trevor Jordache's burial ground.

Where a scene does not have the backdrop of one of the show's own regular sets, the writer needs to conjure the flavour of the surroundings as clearly and concisely as possible. Naturally, if the setting for the scene is only new or different in terms of the show but is, in essence, a commonly experienced environment such as a hospital, courtroom, airport or whatever, the writer need not waste time on describing it. Dentists' waiting rooms, for instance, are pretty much of a muchness unless they are, at one of end of the spectrum, very privately plush or, at the other end, catering to the deeply deprived – and even then they can be summed-up in a sentence. If the situation calls for the *average* waiting room, it matters more that the writer transmit what their characters are doing and feeling rather than the background against which they are doing it.

To illustrate, let's take a scene set in a hospital. Since the show's budget will dictate whether the ICU is a real one on location or a mock-up created on campus, there is no point in the writer describing everything down to the colour of the walls.

<u>Sc.8798.03   (INT.)   HOSPITAL   DAY</u>

THE INTENSIVE CARE UNIT. WAYNE LIES UNCONSCIOUS. <u>DOLORES</u>, ASHEN WITH WORRY, SITS WATCHING THE BLEEPING MONITORS AROUND THE BED. SHE COVERS HER FACE WITH HER HANDS TRYING TO RUB EXHAUSTION FROM HER EYES.

OOV WE HEAR THE VOICE OF <u>DR SHAW</u>.

<u>DOCTOR SHAW</u>: (GENTLY) Mrs Dent.

<u>DOLORES</u> DOESN'T SEEM TO HEAR. <u>DR SHAW</u> COMES INTO VIEW AND PUTS A CAREFUL HAND ON HER SHOULDER.

<u>DOLORES</u> LOOKS UP AT HIM IN ALARM.

<u>DOLORES</u>: Have they got the results?

It obviously calls for a slightly different approach to the scene intro when Soap characters are taken into a situation that is neither standard to the show nor generally familiar to the audience. And this situation can arise both when a scene or scenes are to be shot away from the studio or production campus, i.e. on location, or when a studio/campus area is to be dressed to represent an unusual setting. If the Producer has asked for scenes with an unusual location-setting, the writer will sometimes be given the opportunity to visit the place/site/building/institution before they begin to write. Having acquainted themselves with the locale, the writer is then better equipped to utilise the background within the scene rather than use it merely as a backdrop to dialogue and action that could have taken place anywhere. This familiarisation also means that, right from scene-intro stage, the writer is able to paint a picture for the Director, actors and production crew – who will most probably not get to visit the actual place until late in the rehearsal stage.

Where the scene/scenes are to be shot against an unfamiliar setting mocked-up on campus, the writer would use the scene intro to suggest not only how they envisage elements of the physical features of set-dressing, but also hopefully to create the atmosphere exuded by the place for the Director and actors from their very first reading of the script.

In either case, the need to draw a fuller picture of any novel Soap background isn't a licence for the writer to indulge in diffuse detail or to rhapsodise. Keeping the maxim 'less is more' in mind, and finding one word that is truly evocative instead of ten effusive ones, is the key to writing a useful scene intro.

Beyond describing the place when it's new, or taking for granted a familiar backdrop, what the short prelude to any scene should do is enable the Director and actors to envisage in an instant what the characters are engaged in doing as we join them. It should also convey a sense of their disposition. If we take the earlier example of DOLORES IS DASHING TO AND FRO SETTING THE TABLE, we know what she is doing but not what frame of mind she is in. She could be rushing in a maternally efficient way, be in a mood of happy anticipation or feel harrassed, nervously excited or even fearful. Putting the reader – be they script editor, director or actor – instantly *into* Dolores' frame of mind, instead of putting them to the time-wasting trouble of having to read on to find out what it might be, is a simple matter of inserting the apposite word or two. For example, EARTH MOTHER DOLORES IS DASHING TO AND FRO; A FRAUGHT DOLORES. . . ; DOLORES, CLUMSY WITH ANXIETY, IS DASHING TO AND FRO. . . Going beyond the apposite word or two is neither necessary nor helpful. As a bad example, the following would be going a dozen words over the top: A DESPERATELY TIRED DOLORES IS, DESPITE HER INNERMOST FEELINGS OF GRIEVOUS HURT, DISAPPOINTMENT AND DEEP FOREBODING, DRIVING HERSELF INTO DASHING TO AND FRO. . .

The other job of a scene intro is to create expectation and/or curiosity about what is to follow. The better the writer is able to transmit the required degree of expectation and curiosity to the Director and actors, the quicker they can get to grips with the material and the more chance there is that they will go on to engage the audience.

In the example given below, for instance, the fact that Dolores' actions are hurried is sufficient to denote that she is running late and that her attitude to the slothful Desmond is potentially somewhat strained. Before a word is spoken, the audience will be anticipating possible conflict.

Sc. 101   INT.   DENTS' SITTING ROOM   DAY

DOLORES is hurriedly donning her coat. A sleepy DESMOND trudges in carrying the morning paper. He is wearing pyjamas.

Note: Even where the same set is used again or repeatedly in an episode, the writer needs to indicate at the top of each new scene the precise point at which we join the action as well stipulating the kind of atmosphere we are joining.

MOOD NOTES or QUALIFYING DIRECTIONS
These are used both before and during the dialogue, for example:

DOLORES: (CONFIDENT) It won't be like that.
or
DESMOND: I'll stay then. (TENDERLY) Take care.

As a general rule, when writing for television, this type of stage direction is bracketed and usually appears in capital letters. When it comes to writing for radio it is more usual for the actors' mood notes to be typed in lower case (normal sentence case) as opposed to capitals, although they are still placed in parenthesis:

(OUTDOORS. CLAMOUR OF FUNFAIR)
PETER: Dodgems next?
CONNIE: (surprised and delighted) Do you mean it?

Again, there is a fine line between giving so many mood notes that it insults the actors and not giving enough to make the character's tone clear. On the whole, a well-written line of dialogue should convey the intention clearly enough for the Director and actor to sense how the line was meant to be delivered, but this can be more easily misread where the actual meaning of the words contrasts with the mood, for example:

DOLORES: (TEASING) I hate you.

Even when writing Soap where, as already discussed, some extra guidelines can be helpful, it is still advisable for the writer to err on the side of caution by giving clear mood notes at the start of the scene and then not repeating them too often until and unless the mood changes, for example:

DOLORES: I can't remember when I last laughed as much.

DESMOND: It's been a great day out, hasn't it? (SUDDENLY BUSINESSLIKE) So? Do you think we could make a go of it in Blackpool?

DOLORES: (SOBERING) I don't know. Living there's not the same, is it?

DIRECTIONS SPECIFYING ACTION

These can appear within a speech or between one piece of dialogue and the next, for example:

DOLORES: I'm sorry. (SHE PULLS BACK FROM HIM) I shouldn't have done that.

DESMOND TURNS AWAY FROM HER. WAYNE STARTS OUT OF THE ROOM, WOUNDED ON HIS MOTHER'S BEHALF.

WAYNE: She only wanted to kiss you goodnight.

Just as important as setting the scene from the outset, is a clear description of how the writer wants the scene to close. This matters particularly in Soap where, even within the space of one episode, the audience has to be given good reason to stay in touch with a whole procession of characters and situations.

What follows are a couple of examples of scene-closing stage directions that would stand a good chance of surviving in the audience's consciousness. The first is the kind of visual television close that would create audience anticipation of further action; the second closes a radio scene with the promise of more emotional character interaction to come later on in the episode.

(*Television scene close*)

DOLORES CARRIES THE BOX TOWARDS THE STOCKROOM.

ON THE UNGUARDED COUNTERTOP TILL.

CUT TO:

(*Radio scene close*)

SALLY: I don't understand what you're trying to say?

BILL: (ominously) I think you do, Sal.

SALLY: (rising hurt) No, that's not good enough. I want you to spell it out. (pause) Well?

Fade.

A HUSH FALLS OVER THE CLEARING

The stage directions that signify brief silences before or during a speech are usually written as (PAUSE) or (BEAT). There are no hard and fast rules about which should be used where, but I tend to think of them as having distinct jobs. Where a question is unexpected and the character has to formulate an answer, my own inclination would be to opt for (PAUSE).

DOLORES: Your mother isn't expecting to stay for tea, is she?

DESMOND: Tea? (PAUSE) I've honestly no idea.

Where the character knows the answer full well but thinks it may be unpalatable, or where there needs to be a sense of the character having something to hide, using (BEAT) seems to me to hit the right note of hesitation.

58

DESMOND: Are you saying you don't love me anymore?

DOLORES: (BEAT) I suppose I am.

or

CONNIE: Have you been seeing Naomi?

PHIL: (BEAT) What makes you think that?

(BEAT) also seems to be more commonly used within a speech where the character is finding it painful to relate an experience, or where they are having difficulty in expressing their feelings.

JILL: He just came at me. The first I knew was (BEAT) when I hit the floor.

or

CONNIE: The first time I saw the baby I felt (BEAT) like it had nothing to do with me.

ALL ACTION AND NO TALK

Of course, the television writer's handling of stage directions is never more crucial than where a scene is composed entirely of action. In the following *Brookside* extract, writer Val Windsor ably demonstrates the art of maintaining visual dramatic thrust and transmitting a character's thoughts and feelings without the use of a single word of dialogue.

Sc. 03   (INT.)   DRUGS HOUSE   DAY

AS ESTABLISHED IN Sc. 01.

RON IS NOW STANDING LOOKING THROUGH THE WINDOW. HE HOLDS UP THE DIRTY, TATTERED BIT OF CLOTH USED AS A CURTAIN TO PEER OUT AT THE STREET.

JIMMY SURFACES SLIGHTLY. HE STIRS AND MAKES A HALF COUGH/HALF CHOKING NOISE. RON TURNS.

JIMMY OPENS HIS EYES. HE IS HARDLY ABLE TO FOCUS. HE THINKS HE SEES RON, BUT IT MAY BE PART OF SOME NIGHTMARE. HIS EYES CLOUD WITH FEAR. HE TRIES TO SAY SOMETHING.

WE HEAR THE WAIL OF AN APPROACHING AMBULANCE.

<u>RON</u> MAKES NO EFFORT TO HELP <u>JIMMY</u>. <u>JIMMY'S</u> ATTEMPT TO SPEAK ENDS IN A FRIGHTENING CHOKING NOISE. HIS EYES FLUTTER AND CLOSE. HE GOES INTO A BRIEF CONVULSION, AND THEN GOES LIMP.

THE AMBULANCE IS COMING CLOSER. ON WHICH...

<u>CUT TO:</u>

Speech numbers

Depending on the Soap, some producers like the writer to provide speech numbers to the left of characters' names, for example:

1. DOLORES: I told you about it, sweetheart.

2. DESMOND: I don't think so.

Radio scripts for *The Archers* do have speech numbers, but they come after the characters' names.

SHULA 1   Tickles, doesn't it?

DANIEL 2   Yes, it does!

The purpose of numbering each speech is for easy reference during draft stages – 'Page 3, Speech 4. Did you seriously mean Dolores calls him "sweetheart"!?' And later to make the Director's life easier during rehearsal – 'Page 5, Speech 2? Don't ask me, darling. I didn't write the bloody thing.' If you are required to supply speech numbers, the form is that they begin from 1 again at the top of each page of the script.

Scene breakdowns

Again, depending on the Producer's preference, a writer may be asked to preface each script they submit with a scene breakdown. As opposed to the allotment of characters, sets and scenes that was supplied with the storyline, the writer's scene breakdown is of the episode as they have written it.

Collating a writer's scene breakdown is a simple matter of going through the finished script in order to make a list under the following headings:

SCENE	I/E	LOCATION	PPS	D/N	CHARACTERS
1265.01	INT.	DENT LIVING RM	1–3	DAY	DOLORES/DESMOND
1265.02	INT.	HARGROVE BCK. BEDRM	4–5	DAY	SUSAN
1265.03	EXT.	DENT REAR PATIO	6–9	DAY	DOLORES/WAYNE/ DESMOND

And so on. If the episode is split by a commercial break, you should indicate where the break will come by inserting END OF PART ONE between the relevant scenes.

The main purpose of creating this breakdown is that it provides the Script Editor and Producer with upfront reassurance that the writer has not deviated from the number of scenes, sets and characters they were allotted as well as giving them an overview of the general balance and movement of the piece. The breakdown sheet is also useful at the first-draft meeting stage as a quick page and scene reference for any points the Producer and/or Script Editor wishes to make.

Writing – some Soap custom and practice

Monologues

Except in special cases as agreed with the Producer, avoid writing hugely long monologues. Alan Bennett may very well have used the device to brilliant effect, but within the single play. Soaps, on the other hand, need characters to express themselves in a more condensed fashion if all the storylines and characters in the episode are to be afforded their fair weight.

In practical terms, protracted speeches are also asking a lot of Soap actors who are generally afforded scant rehearsal time. It also has to be taken into account that they may well be rehearsing one script while recording another that has got further up the production line.

Stay with the storyline

Resist the temptation to change agreed storylines. If, part-way through your script, you have an earth-shattering idea that didn't strike you at the story conference, you must contact the Producer. If he or she agrees to the change, that's fine. Otherwise, stick religiously to the given plot because any alteration you make will invariably have knock-on effects in your fellow writers' scripts. It may also have a knock-on effect as far as the next block of storylines is concerned.

Dialect

Stick to whatever the custom is when it comes to how much or how little of the dialogue is written colloquially and/or in regional accents. A script littered with heavy dialect can be very clumsy to read. Regular actors will be well enough immersed in the character they play not to need every word signposted. If a script contains a new character, it is usually enough to indicate in the qualifying directions to their first speech that they speak with a heavy Birmingham, or whatever, accent.

Two-hander scenes

Try to plan your episode so that you do not end up with too many two-hander scenes – and where you have to have them, try not to have them running consecutively. No more than a couple of people in too many scenes can make for a static, not to mention sparse look to an episode. Given that you will have a lot of action and information to set against a limited number of sets and locations, you can usually find opportunities to segue other stories and characters into a scene.

This isn't to say that characters should ever be hauled into a scene simply as a prop to stop it being a two-hander. If you put a character into a scene you must use them effectively. Have them dumbly languishing in the background, and it's odds-on they won't survive the first draft.

Children

Unless they are absolutely central to a storyline, avoid giving child actors too much to do. This isn't a question of their acting ability, it is because there are, quite properly, strict limitations on the number of hours that younger cast-members are allowed to work. In addition to the difficulties the Director will have in trying to manoeuvre around this time restriction, children will almost certainly have to be accompanied by, or supplied with, a chaperone for both rehearsals and recordings.

'Allo-allo'
Avoid 'echo' dialogue:

> DOLORES: She could be pregnant.
>
> DESMOND: What do you mean, she could be pregnant?
>
> DOLORES: I mean she could be pregnant.
>
> DESMOND: You're saying she could be pregnant?

While in reality we often repeat what someone has said in order to give ourselves time to absorb the information, or to signify shock or disbelief, there is seldom room for the device of repetition in a Soap episode. Every line in Soap has to work hard for its living and move smartly on from information to reaction.

Yeah, right, well, look, listen, know what I mean?
Avoid starting speeches with 'Look' or 'Listen': scripts can end up littered with them and actors tend to put them in anyway. 'You know' and 'like' (as in 'I did see her, like') can also get tagged on here and there by the actors, so it's better if the writer uses them sparingly to stop the whole thing becoming hopelessly repetitive – know what I mean?

Don't put the right words in the wrong mouth
If Dolores tends to be the monosyllabic sort, don't start embellishing her speeches. She may have something emotionally complicated or deeply philosophical to transmit, but it's up to the writer to translate the thought into how she would say it. This doesn't mean that she has to say it less well. An inarticulate character deserves every bit as much, if not more, of the writer's inventiveness when it comes to giving them a means of expression. Making someone say something that matters, that is insightful or moving, using only that character's limited vocabulary is one of the more creative challenges of Soap writing – so it's a pity, not to mention a dereliction, to cop out.

Worried – or is it just wind?

One way in which writers can be tempted to cop out is to abandon speech altogether and opt for relying entirely on facial expression to convey the character's emotion. This is rarely, if ever, a good idea. Consider those short rehearsal times and the invariably crammed content of the episode which combine into the televisual truism that subtlety will more often than not get lost in translation. What's described in the stage directions as a look of deep despair can end up looking on screen like nothing more meaningful than a suppressed fart. And it will not be the actor's or the Director's fault if the writer has relied on silence to do the work of a few well-chosen words.

Quite apart from its potential for simply looking naff on screen, leaving it all to 'the look' also runs the risk of misleading the actor, Director, and ultimately the audience in terms of continuity. It could be crucial to future plotlines that, in one episode, Desmond reacts in a very specific way to a particular situation. The actor may not know this yet, since he isn't aware of upcoming story-lines, but if what he conveys gets misinterpreted it may make a nonsense of events somewhere down the line. If in doubt, go for a belt-and-braces job and reinforce the spoken emotion with a supplementary stage direction as to the facial expression.

Keep the characters 'in character'

People often ask how it is possible for a host of different writers to maintain such seamless consistency when it comes to the manner in which Soap characters speak and express themselves. The writers do have a head start, of course, in that experienced Soap actors have so successfully immersed themselves in their Soap alter-ego that what the writer feeds into an actor's actual self is skilfully processed to emerge through the mouth of their fictional character. It obviously makes it far harder for actors to do this if the writer endlessly provides words and speech mannerisms that strike discordant notes as far as their Soap character is concerned.

This is where the writerly attribute of being a good listener needs to be honed above and beyond the general sense. Each person, even if they share the same regional accent, has individual accents and rhythms to their speech; idiosyncracies in the way they pause and punctuate, elect emphasis and so on. The writer needs to know each of the characters' individual voices well enough to 'hear' them in their head as they write the dialogue.

Since it's important in any form of writing to be able to 'hear voices' – the voices of the characters you are endeavouring to bring to life – it's useful for new writers to practise tuning their antennae when it comes to being able to recognise and reproduce speech patterns. A simple way of starting to sharpen this faculty is to take more than a passing interest in any snatch of conversation overheard on the bus, in the supermarket queue or from the next table in the pub. The subject of the exchange needn't be of any particular significance; any everyday bit of banter will do. As soon as you get the chance, try to reproduce what you heard. It doesn't matter if it isn't a verbatim account of the conversation. What matters is that you recall enough of the major speech characteristics to be able to 'hear' the participants as you report the kernel of what they said.

As the next step in the exercise, invent a different conversation to take place between those same people. In effect you are using the same instruments to play a different tune. If you retained the sound of those instruments well enough, you will find you can concentrate on the substance of what you are concocting for them to say – while the way in which they would say it comes naturally to your inner ear.

Naturalistic dialogue

As you hone your innate listening ability – or learn to develop this essential tool – by eavesdropping on actual conversations, it'll be hard not to notice how informal and grammatically rule-breaking most everyday speech is. In Soap writing, where the job is to create recognisable everyday characters, it's as well not to let syntax get in the way of a good sentence. Creating a speech that is grammatically pure may prove you are a fine philologist, but it won't matter how right the sentence is if it sounds wrong coming out of the character's mouth.

If in doubt as to whether a speech you have written would come out sounding stilted and artificial, simply read it aloud yourself with your character's voice in mind. If it sounds more like Dolores is making a speech to the Society for the Preservation of Pedantry rather than passing the time of day with the postman, you need to hit the delete key.

You say tomato, I say erubescent edible fruit

Just as Soap writing is not an opportunity to prove your grammatical expertise, neither is it the place for flaunting an exotic vocabulary. As in all other forms of writing, it is easy to hinder the pace and obscure the basic intent by substituting fancy words for good old-fashioned plain ones.

When the writer, whether driven by boredom or conceit, uses an obscure alternative to the obvious word, it will invariably clutter rather than clarify. Finding an uncommon word is not the same as having an individual voice as a writer. Because a word has novelty value it does not necessarily serve to express the writer's meaning more exactly. What it's more likely to do is prove that the writer has absolutely nothing new to say and is trying to disguise the fact by saying the same stale old thing in a new way. What does make for a singular writer is the range and quality of perspective and insight that they weave into the everyday stuff of vocabulary.

Scene construction

Whether long or short, light or dark, a Soap scene will invariably be expected to do three fundamental jobs. These are:

a) To remind or tell the audience where we've been.
b) To tell the viewer something new about where we are.
c) To create curiosity about where next.

Where've we been?

The insistence on a) is often the subject of irritation to writers who feel hard-pressed to fit b) and c) into the short span of an episode. Why, they complain, is it necessary to waste time going over old ground? Because, as the Producer will point out, strange as it may seem to the writers – whose whole existence is centred around their Soap's storylines – the audience has other calls on its attention. However faithful the fans, it is not safe to assume that every last one of them is up to speed on every jot and tittle of every single storyline. It is also desirable to win new audience members and it helps if they have at least some background to latch on to.

The goal then is to get the audience to invest in a storyline they may have come to late in the run or as complete strangers – *and* to get them to re-invest scene-by-scene in what is only one of several other storylines grappling for their attention. The trick is to do it without it sticking out further than the proverbial sore thumb.

In radio writing, leaden-footed exposition is summed up by, 'The revolver I am holding in my right hand is loaded.' The ham-fisted television Soap equivalent of explaining where we're at would go something like this:

DOLORES: How can you say that when you know very well how hard I've been struggling? What with your dad losing his job because of him starting to get arthritis and then his next boss sacking him for stealing from work when he'd never do such a thing in a million years, and then with him having a nervous breakdown after he'd gone and knocked that little poor girl down and put her in a coma, I've been at my wit's end.

As, no doubt, any audience would be in the unlikely event that such a speech escaped the Script Editor's scalpel. Much thought and skill needs to go into any necessary exposition if it isn't to come out as patronising or ridiculous as the above. For a start it helps not to have all the information coming out of one character's mouth. The following is still handled with pretty broad strokes, since normally there would be a whole scene or set of scenes throughout which the back-referencing information could be more light-handedly dabbed, but it may stand to illustrate the point:

DOLORES: How can you say that? You know how I've struggled since your dad lost his job.

WAYNE: It was unfair dismissal, that. Just because he got arthritis.

DOLORES: Wouldn't have mattered if his next job had worked out. (DISBELIEVINGLY) Stealing from work? Your dad?! (SHAKES HEAD) No wonder he was in a state the day he knocked that kiddie down.

WAYNE: (SADLY) I suppose putting a kid in a coma would be enough to drive most people nuts.

DOLORES: (UPSET/REPRIMANDING) Your Dad's not nuts. It's a nervous breakdown.

The two versions contain the same number of words, carry all the necessary information and convey the same meaning, but I think you'll agree the second serves it up in a much more palatable fashion.

What's new?

The second job of the scene is to tell the audience something new about the situation. If we take the dialogue above which was composed of exposition, we now need to move the story on a step further. Of course, it would depend on the storyline as to what the next twist in the plot was going to be, but let's say the storyline breakdown calls for Dolores to reveal that Desmond is coming home from his stay in hospital. The scene could proceed as follows:

DOLORES: (UPSET/REPRIMANDING) Your Dad's not nuts. It's a nervous breakdown. I hope you're going to be more careful about your language when he comes home tomorrow.

WAYNE: (SHOCKED) Tomorrow? But I only saw him yesterday and he could hardly stop crying!

DOLORES: It'll take time – they've said that.

What next?

Let's assume that in the storyline breakdown for the episode it states that Wayne leaves home and that that event has been designated as the hook of the episode. In an earlier scene or scenes such as the one we are building, the writer can wind up the ante a notch at a time towards Wayne's final outburst and departure. In this one we begin to signal that there is jeopardy in the situation:

WAYNE: But they should keep him 'til he's better.

DOLORES: They need the bed. And anyway he'll get better faster at home.

WAYNE: But he doesn't want people seeing him like that.

DOLORES: (REALISING WAYNE'S CONCERN IS FOR HIMSELF) You mean *you* don't. It's not going to help if he sees you thinking he's some sort of embarrassment.

WAYNE: (DEFENSIVE ANGER) I never said that. (STARTING TO LEAVE) But I might have known you'd think it.

          ON <u>DOLORES</u> ANXIOUS ABOUT THE RIFT DESMOND'S RETURN IS ALREADY CAUSING.

<u>CUT TO:</u>

In a subsequent scene, the build towards the dénouement can continue:

          <u>CONNIE</u> IS HELPING <u>DOLORES</u> TO PUSH AN ARMCHAIR CLOSER TO THE WINDOW. <u>WAYNE</u> COMES IN.

WAYNE: (OF ARMCHAIR) I can't see the telly with it there.

DOLORES: We just thought it'd be nicer for your Dad.

          CONNIE MOVES A SIDE-TABLE NEXT TO THE ARMCHAIR AND THEN STARTS OUT INTO THE HALL.

CONNIE: I'll just get those car mags I brought for him.

          <u>DOLORES</u> FUSSES ABOUT MOVING A PLANT ON THE WINDOW SILL. <u>WAYNE</u> LOOKS LONG-SUFFERING.

DOLORES: There. He should be able to see out now.

WAYNE: But Dad's not going to be able to see the telly from there either.

DOLORES: He'll not be watching it. The hospital said he'll need quiet.

WAYNE: (APPALLED) For how long?

DOLORES: (WEARILY) For as long as it takes.

69

>CONNIE COMES IN ON THE STRAINED ATMOSPHERE. SHE GOES TO PUT THREE CAR MAGAZINES ON THE SIDE TABLE.

DOLORES: (TO CONNIE) Thanks, love.

CONNIE: Got them on the way back from the ante-natal.

DOLORES: Everything okay?

>CONNIE STARTS TO SHOVE THE SOFA AWAY FROM THE NEWLY POSITIONED ARMCHAIR.

CONNIE: Fine. Blood pressure's up a bit. (DOLORES LOOKS CONCERNED – CONNIE SMILES) It's fine – honest – nothing to worry about.

DOLORES: (TO WAYNE) Help your sister with that.

>WAYNE GRUDGINGLY NUDGES THE SOFA ALONG WITH HIS KNEE.

WAYNE: But why do you have to move everything now? He's not home 'til tomorrow and the match is going to be on any minute.

CONNIE: (SHRUGS) So? Go watch it round at Tim's.

>WAYNE GROANS.

DOLORES: (APPEALING TO WAYNE) It'll only be for a while. And it's not going to help if your Dad's feels like he's some sort of nuisance.

CONNIE: (MUTTERING IRRITABLY) It's not Dad that's the nuisance.

WAYNE: (ANGRY/STARTING TO LEAVE) Be better if I stay out of the way then, won't it?

CONNIE: Where are you going?

WAYNE: (OOV AS HE SHOUTS BACK FROM THE HALL) Tim's!

DOLORES: (WORRIED/CALLING AFTER HIM) But you'll be back for your supper, won't you?

>CONNIE AND DOLORES HEAR THE FRONT DOOR SLAM AND EXCHANGE A LOOK OF FRUSTRATION.

CONNIE: Don't worry – he'll be back.

ON <u>DOLORES</u>, LOOKING LESS THAN CERTAIN.

CUT TO:

The scene has achieved its three aims: it has reminded the audience of the story so far, told us something new about the progress of Connie's pregnancy (dropping a hint at possible future problems), and what Wayne saw as the conspiracy of disregard by the women has alienated him still further. When Wayne returns for the supper scene – or, better still, if he is late for supper – the situation is nicely set to reach its dénouement of the son leaving home on the eve of his father's return.

Now you've written it, read it

There's a lot to take account of in writing an episode of Soap, and it's easy to forget that what you are trying to achieve is not simply a satisfactory schematic arrangement but a satisfying piece of drama.

I once emerged from the spare bedroom – grandly referred to as my office – pale from screen irradiation but proud to have completed three half-hour episodes in just over two weeks. Was I pleased with them, my partner asked. 'Dunno,' I said, 'I haven't read 'em.' And it was only then that I realised that I hadn't. I had created the structure, navigated my way through all the plot points, sweated over the dialogue in each and every separate scene, but I frankly had no idea of how any of those three episodes would 'feel' to someone coming at them as anything but an exercise in logistics.

One of the first things you learn about any form of writing is that the work always benefits from being set aside for a while. Authors often speak of finishing a play or a novel and putting it away in a drawer for six months or even a year before re-reading it. Only then can they separate themselves from the actual process of writing and gauge the piece from a gut-reaction perpective. The overall flow and pace of a piece is also easier to assess when the writer has had some time to stand back. It's obviously impossible to become as complete a stranger to the work as any audience would be, but this proving time can bring the writer closer to seeing their creation – warts and all.

The Soap process, of course, can't allow for the luxury of leaving a script aside for any length of time. The writer must carve out of the short allotment of writing time whatever slender gap they can between finishing the script and submitting it. Whatever else can't be managed by way of distancing, leave at least enough time to print up a hard copy of the script and sit down and read it (*see* also pp. 113–21 on *Rewrites*). There may not be any time left to make alterations to the first draft at this stage, but you at least stand a chance of clocking a few of the potential criticisms that the Script Editor/Producer may have and be in a position to offer up your own ideas for changes or improvements.

A time to savour

Few writing remits are as tightly governed as Soap. Even fewer are as satisfying when, somehow, it all comes together. And, yes, of course it's hard work but that doesn't mean it needs to be seen as a grind. In fact, if it feels more like grind than good honest graft during the writing, that will probably end up coming across on screen. As with any writing, the hard work shouldn't show. With Soap writing, all the mechanics and constituents that need to be taken into account do become second nature, allowing the writer to enjoy inventing drama and dialogue.

At any rate, on the day the script goes off in the post, the two or three weeks of grey-matter-bashing graft seem as nothing – a hard labour soon forgotten in the face of what it's produced. The first draft is done and delivered on time. Revels of the quietly reflective, mainly moderate or insanely jolly sort are in order, as is a re-introduction to family, friends and life in general.

Nothing can mar the moment – the brief moment before joy starts becoming a little more confined as the reality of what's been achieved so far sinks in along with the meaning of those two little words: First Draft.

5. More Soap Ingredients

Apart from techniques covered so far, there are other factors that can impact, either directly or indirectly, on how the writer approaches a Soap script.

Actors. Bless

Blow all these boring meetings with behind-the-scenes folk and all this writing-technique stuff. There is another question frequently asked of Soap writers: do you ever get to meet *the actors*? It's not polite to reply 'Only if I'm not very careful,' so it's best to stick to smiling and nodding as if still overcome at having shared the canteen salad-prongs with Dolores.

As to the enquiry that often comes hot on the heels – 'What are they *like*?' – I've found actors to be as absolutely ordinary as the rest of us while being just as definitely a breed apart. As individuals they come in the same varying degrees of niceness as the non-thespian population, and range from gloriously eccentric to less interesting than the local butcher.

It's sometimes harder than with most other people to know if you know them or not – if you know what I mean. Actors have to constantly form and re-form instantaneous relationships with members of the company they are working and living hugger-mugger with for the duration of a play, film or whatever. Without this facility for instant integration it would be impossible to achieve the varied but convincing degrees of intimacy they're required to play out. Whether transience is an occupational hazard to which they have had to adapt, or an innate characteristic to which they have fitted a profession, is hard to say. Whichever, for us more sedentary sorts, these kisses, coos and cuddles from a complete stranger can come as something of a surprise. Just as it can be disconcerting to be treated one minute to their total focus only to find in the next that their fascinated eyeline has drifted somewhere over your shoulder onto someone more interesting. Or perhaps just more useful. It'd be unfair to condemn this trip-switch attention span, since around 90% of the acting fraternity are out of work at any one time and networking needs to come as naturally as drawing breath.

There's only one star

Don't get me wrong, most actors are sensitive, intelligent, generous, conscientious, unpretentious human beings. And those who aren't usually don't last long in Soap. This is because Soap isn't ultimately a star vehicle: it is the star.

Soap can and regularly does bring unknowns to prominence, providing talented ingenues and clever old troopers alike with enough exposure to turn them into ratings-worthy, even poachable 'names'. But Soap itself can't afford to depend for its survival on any one celebrity. The show, as they say, must go on despite the death or departure of any single character – no matter how long-running and adored a fixture they have become. And it always does go on. No-one knows this – subliminally or for sure – better than the actors themselves, and this sense of their own Soap mortality stops most Soap actors' egos from over-inflating to any degree that would make them unmanageable.

I've got this really great idea

In fact, in any other circumstance than being one of the people who writes their Soap parts, actors mostly make excellent company. Trouble is, when you are one of the people providing their material, some of them can want to bend your ear in ways that are not necessarily helpful.

It's not unusual in Soap corridors, canteens and at festive knees-ups to see a writer pinioned in wide-eyed panic by an actor giving them the benefit of a 'brill idea' they've had for a storyline. Sometimes calling for a budget that Spielberg would blench at, sometimes more, what these story suggestions always have in common is that the actor whose idea it is would have to be in it. A lot. In fact, all the time for the several weeks, months if not years it would most certainly run. These waylayings of writers have a tendency to happen more just before any conference that actors have got wind of and at which, rumour has it, cast changes are to be discussed. Acting being every bit as precarious a way of making a living as writing, it isn't hard to sympathise with a professional trying to keep his or her name uppermost on the list of those who should be kept on board. And should they be kept on board, it is obviously in their best interest to be given more and meatier stuff to do.

Writing for the character

Unfortunately, as mentioned earlier, sympathy and subsequent favouritism can be a dangerous commodity. Writers, however much they like or rate an actor, are not writing for them; they are writing for the character they play. It might well benefit the show overall if a particular character takes a back seat or moves on altogether. And knowing and caring about an actor on too personal a level can skew a writer's judgement when it comes to any involvement they have in such decisions.

Of course, actors are constitutionally adept at not identifying to a dangerous degree with the parts they play but, just occasionally, they can show a tendency to blur the line between how their screen character is perceived and how they would like their own persona to come across. Again, it can be a problem for the writer if he or she knows, for example, that Connie who plays Dolores hates her character coming over as weak. Connie may very well have a terrific story idea for how Dolores transforms herself into an assertive new woman, but to take the character down that route may not be for the good of the show.

One of the most difficult on-screen personas to get an actor to sustain over a period of time is that of the villain. Most love to exercise their dramatic muscles on playing the baddie for a while but it is, after all, human nature to want to be liked and gradually an actor can begin to try to soften their character. It's up to the writing team to notice when this is happening and, if it is in the show's interest that Desmond goes on being the louse he's always been, to give the actor less leeway for turning his character into a cuddlier soul.

A different kind of pitfall worth watching out for is where the character *doesn't* change after what, on screen, has been some life-changing event. The fast turn-around of Soap stories can leave scant space in which to register emotional realignments and altered values following traumas or upheavals. If the writers are awake to this potential hazard they can build in, at the very least, some indications that the character has been affected, thus lessening the risk of them seeming unnaturally phlegmatic, not to say pathologically detached.

Keeping the actors' lot in mind

Given the nature of the genre, Soap actors, like the writers, can't always be given full reign when it comes to individual creativity. Dialogue tends to be sacrosanct because of the ramifications any alteration could have on upcoming storylines, and tight rehearsal schedules often leave an actor frustrated about not having had time to polish a performance to its peak. It's another of the minor Soap miracles that so often, so many of them overcome these constraints to turn in such splendidly convincing stuff.

It's worth repeating that the writer can help by not giving an actor huge, convoluted wodges of dialogue which they will have scant time to learn and perfect. It's probably kindest too to remember that writers write and actors act, which means not stipulating that Desmond and Dolores ad-lib in the background of a scene. If it matters to the scene to see them engaged in dialogue behind the main action, then it matters that they portray the appropriate expressions and body language. Better then to provide them with words – even though the words, if they're heard at all, will only be background noise.

Lost for words

By something of the same token, it tends not to be a good idea to leave actors bereft of words halfway through a sentence. The dot-dot-dot device ('What do you think you are. . . ?') often doesn't work as the writer envisaged. Actors under pressure have a tendency to see the first dot as a full stop, so instead of the writer's intention – which was a foreshortened 'What do you think you are doing?' – you could get, 'What do you think you are?'

Putting the final desired word in brackets after the dots – 'What do you think you are. . . (doing)?' – may sometimes stop the speech sounding like it died suddenly rather than dried in the heat of the moment, but by far the safest way is to give the actor the complete speech and let them sever the sense of it wherever it feels most natural in performance.

Right words, wrong emphasis

It goes without saying that the majority of actors can be trusted to transmit the writer's intended meaning most of the time. But again, given the frantic pace of Soap schedules, it pays to try to second-guess where it might all go awry. Keeping in mind how many different ways the same sentence can be said can save the writer much disappointment, not to mention despair, when they see their episode transmitted.

For example, if what the actor is provided with is a totally casual speech, such as 'I didn't know you were going to see Dolores,' it can end up coming off the page with a wholly different meaning altogether:

'*I* didn't know you were going to see Dolores.'

or

'I didn't know you were going to see *Dolores*.'

or

'I didn't know *you* were going to see Dolores.'

Or it can carry half-a-dozen other connotations depending upon which of the other six words the actor opts to lean on. Try it and you'll see how easy it is to alter the meaning and tone of what was intended to be a passing remark.

Clear mood notes and stage directions (*see* also Chapter 4) can help prevent sentences sounding odd, confusing or – more dangerously, since this is Soap – misleading to the audience, but there is no way to rule misreadings out altogether and so the writer just has to learn to live with the occasional one.

Keeping characters consistent

Actors – aided by an inattentive director – can confound the writer and confuse the audience without even opening their mouths. Since their involvement in a run of episodes may be sporadic, they have been known to appear in a scene looking inappropriately happy or unaccountably miserable. This is because nobody has reminded them that the episode they last recorded involved seeing them in a particular emotional state. It's a real danger where their story strand isn't being featured specifically in the episode they are currently recording – and where it has been taken for granted that they will go on transmitting their joy or gloom or whatever in the background. The trouble is that in between recording what was their last episode and what will, on screen, be the next, the actor may well have had time off, been to a read-through for a future episode and be in the middle of rehearsing yet another one. It is very understandable that he or she might have lost their place in the state-of-mind stakes.

To try to circumvent the scenario whereby Desmond, who was last seen crippled by anxiety, leaps into the following episode without a care in the world, it's helpful if the writer can do the reminding. This is easily done with a mood note or stage direction at the point where the character is first seen in an episode. For example:

DESMOND, STILL SULKING ABOUT HIS DEMOTION, ENTERS AND SITS DOWN.

or

ANGELA, STILL IN HAPPY HONEYMOON MOOD, BOUNCES INTO THE SALON.

The most spectactular piece of actor-character amnesia I've ever come across was impossible to predict. Thankfully, it never reached the screen.

We of the writing team were treated to it in its rough-cut state when an apoplectically angry Producer stormed in and slammed the tape into the meeting-room video. 'First one to spot the deliberate mistake,' he challenged through clenched teeth. The scene in question started bewilderingly well. An expensive location job which, for once, seemed to be justifying all the trouble and cost. The launch party for a new PR firm, bravely headed by one of our major characters remaking her life after illness, looked utterly convincing. The grand venue looked amazing, a larger than usual cast of Extras portraying party-goers weren't doing any silly business in the background, the expensive buffet actually looked lavish, the venue and the characters were all wonderfully dressed. . .

Whoops! Having spent months giving a moving portrayal of a woman who had suffered the misery of a mastectomy and the aftermath of self-consciousness about her mutilated body, our actress had elected to wear something low-cut enough to give her character a *cleavage*!? Yep, there it was – or rather, there *they* were – two unmistakably real breasts.

And no-one except the Producer had spotted it. Not Wardrobe, not the Director, nor any of the dozens of other people on location that day and, most remarkably of all, not the actress herself. Had the Producer blinked in the editing suite, the scene could well have gone out and destroyed the show's credibility in a way it would have been hard to defend. And all for the want of two inches of fabric. Needless to say, that and all the subsequent party scenes that had to be hastily re-shot were not done on anywhere near as generous a budget. From sushi to sausage rolls in one décolletage. But at least it was better than us losing the trust of all those women who had followed and identified with the breast cancer story.

In the enormity of the significance it might have had, this boob (sorry) was, fortunately, rare. But there any many lesser examples where actors have suffered brain-storms and lost sight of how real and consistent their on-screen persona must remain at all times. Midway through playing nigh unto death on screen, actors have returned from a real-life holiday looking like a bronzed god. Why everyone is looking so shell-shocked when they're back and raring to play the next pneumonia scene is a temporary mystery to them. Long locks have been known to do an overnight bunk in favour of shaven-headedness, and beards and moustaches have forever been an all too easily removable feature. It all means someone having to hastily invent a reason, plus some dialogue, to explain the character's unscheduled behaviour, but such small thought-lessnesses are usually forgiven, especially with actors who have been turning in demanding performances over an intensive period.

Going out in style

Given that their life can't be entirely their own once they have adopted a Soap mantle, it's not surprising that some actors eventually buckle at the knees and want out. Torn between the pros of popularity and the cons of becoming type-cast – and often on the horns of the same dilemma as writers when it comes to sticking with the rare security of regular work or casting themselves back out into a cold climate – actors usually take a long time in deciding to leave the safe, if not always satisfactory, world of Soap.

When an actor does decide to make the leap, they may well be doing it because they feel they have not been given enough dramatic or demanding stuff. And they may well be right. But it doesn't help the actor to know that, in some instances, the writers are only too aware of how persistently they've neglected their character. With the best will in the world it can be hard to find space for consistent and substantial development of all the players within such a densely packed product. The writing team could, on the other hand, have become so caught up in nurturing their latest character creation that they've frankly forgotten their duty to sustain some of the earlier ones.

The irony is that a character's departure will invariably concentrate the writers' minds into making the best capital they can out of their going. Having felt – and sometimes having been – consistently under-used, actors find that the writers have been nudged into inventing for them the very sort of powerful, high-profile material they were leaving for the lack of. The actor's performance rises to the occasion, the writers are reminded of how bloody good they are, and there are often regrets on both sides that what becomes a coup de television is, irreversibly, a swansong.

When an actor makes a sudden decision to go, there is sometimes no contractual way to stop them in time for it not to blow a huge hole in already planned or, worse, already written storylines. These unscheduled departures, like those caused by the sadder circumstances of an actor's serious illness or death, can call for some pretty summary unravelling and even swifter rewrites if the lacuna is to be darned. This can be easier said than done depending on how close to transmission the character bows out and how central they were. There is sometimes no option but to stretch the audience's credibility to its limits with devices that under normal circumstances would be laughable.

Nobody knows better than the team of panic-stricken writers that Dolores would no more have upped and abandoned beloved husband, kids and career to go and live with her Auntie Doris in Bangor than fly to the moon – nobody but the audience, that is. But in some cases it's down to the writers just having to trust to the fans' forgiving faithfulness, and the fond hope that the desire to move on as fast as possible is mutual.

Finding their forte

Soap scribes all have their own opinion as to which actors they find a joy to write for and which seem bent on mangling their every syllable. Some actors are loved or loathed by major or minor consensus within the team. Those who are universally held to be bad to write for can last an astonishing length of time. This prolonged and painful state of affairs can come about when a producer thinks he or she has cast dynamite for which the writers have simply failed to find the right fuse. What will ignite his prodigy, the Producer insists, is more comedy. Humour is a seriously difficult thing to write (*see* below) and it's even less of a joke to see it strangled on delivery. The Producer changes tack – more tragedy then. Which *does* have the audience falling about.

The Producer is still convinced that the writers just haven't found the actors' *métier*. More balls, bottle and general aggro is called for: it's more marshmallow than menace. No, no, no! the Producer yells with very convincing menace, the writers just aren't trying hard enough. What will make the character work is allowing the actor to show more softness and sensitivity. . .

And just occasionally it does so happen that the writing team finally hit upon a persona that the poor, now hopelessly confused actor can successfully transfuse into their screen character. In the cases where they never do, it is not the writers' or the actors' fault but the sad consequence of what was, from the outset, a piece of gross miscasting.

However justified or otherwise these judgements of actors' abilities or suitability, they can't ultimately be allowed to matter. Everyone within the ensemble deserves equal regard and it is to actors' credit that, despite this not always being the case, so many of them serve the writers so long and so well.

Light bits

You know the sort of thing I mean: the playful, pranky, terminally jaunty little self-contained storylines that are put there to leaven and lighten what producers think might otherwise be too heavyweight a half-hour. There's a penchant for 'Lite Bitz' too among television news editors – a terrible tendency to suddenly pitch our hearts and minds straight from real human awfulness into some rankly sentimental nonsense. And in this country it's hardly any accident that this good news invariably involves some animal or other. Quick, show 'em a shot of the pig that's been fitted with free contact lenses before they think we're telling 'em the world's a pitiless dungheap.

Oh, no, not Ho-ho-ho

Sobbing enjoyably along to some agonising Soap moment, wide-eyed with suspense, or pulsating to some purple patch, you may well have found yourself unceremoniously heaved into a deeply naff 'ho-ho-ho' interlude, the time-wasting whimsicality of which only doesn't involve animals because of their being notoriously difficult to work with. Not that I have anything against humour in Soaps. As in any other areas of writing, I'm convinced of its value as a scalpel that can slice right down to the bone, as well as being an advocate for its use in sliding home the most serious of points. But that's humour, not farce. Not that I have anything against farce when it's done deftly and in the appropriate place. As, so often on Soaps, it isn't.

What successful humour and farce have in common is a basis in some sort of human truth. As a criterion, truth does keep on popping up, I know. But for those doubting it as the fount of all that's truly funny, I can only suggest taking the matter up with Billy Connolly.

Cut the funny business

Light Bits can be about as far away from the truth as Soap ever gets. They tend to proliferate where too few of the regular characters are allowed to be naturally and consistently amusing on their own account. This, I maintain, tends to be less often the fault of the writers and more often a result of the relentless Soap system. It's easy to see how characters who are not written in a one-dimensional way just end up like that when, if anything has to be cut from a script, it will probably be humour. In a too densely packed script, the Producer will often demand the tightening-up of a character's speeches, and it's the wit-factor that's invariably considered dispensable. In event-heavy episodes, lines that carry plot can't go, information can't go, and the build to a hook can't go without somebody getting shot for it. And even those colourful little idiosyncrasies that escape the Producer's blade may not make it as far as the screen.

On a final Friday night shoot, when the Director's got scenes running over and a crew running into overtime, overboard can go everything from a wry aside to a full-blown joke. If it happens enough the audience will eventually start to squeal and the Producer will start to bang the table. How did the show get to be such a relentless doom-fest? Why isn't there more humour in it!? What ought to follow is some serious debate about integral humour; what all too often does is a Silly Season. The panic measures that it's deemed necessary to take in order to stem the flow of criticism and staunch the haemorrhaging audience figures will invariably involve broad-stroke efforts to brighten things up. In an outbreak of Light Bits, characters are hauled clumsily out of their normal senses to people pantomime plotlines which may in themselves be titter-(or wince)-worthy but seldom bring anything of lasting value to the show as a whole.

For all the ingredients that producers and directors see as crucial to the Soap recipe, the seasoning of humour is most often forgotten.

What can the writer do?

You could remind your Producer that some of the most memorable Soap characters of all time achieved their archive status for the very good reason that actors and writers were given room to imbue them with wit. Not always likeable, sometimes cross-grained or downright reprehensible, these characters could, nevertheless, show us the complexities of human nature even as we chuckled, or make us care about some deeply serious stuff even as we split our sides.

As writers we should cherish the precious few characters currently on our screens who have survived the increasingly plot-driven Soap process with their sense of humour intact – the ones who have escaped being turned into occasional clowns – and try to match the standard.

Funny ha-ha and funny peculiar

In day-to-day life we all know people who set out to amuse as well as those whose characteristics we find amusing in themselves. Both categories benefit from a 'forgivability factor' – that is to say, because we know them, we often laugh at jokes which aren't *that* funny and suffer the funny-peculiar fool if not gladly then with extended patience. We enter into a kind of conspiracy: Uncle Joe's jokes are older than God but we go on convincing him and ourselves that he's funny if we go on laughing. So we do. Just as we conspire to confirm Batty-Nora-next-door's harmlessness to her and to ourselves by enjoying her as lovable old eccentric.

When people are paid to be funny or portray amusing characteristics, we are less inclined to make such allowances. The exceptions are those professional comedians and comic-character actors who struck a funny bone in us at some point in our lives and whom we go on finding funny out of loyalty – loyalty not just to them but to our own judgement. We believed, we invested in the idea that they were funny. If we stop believing it then our investment must have been misplaced. So, just like with good old Uncle Joe, we go on laughing. For the most part, though, the professional funny man or comic-character actor can curry no such favour when it comes to an audience's affections and they live or die on the strength of their material.

It is hard enough in the context of a sitcom to keep funny characters of either the ha-ha or peculiar sort from becoming wearing to the nerves. So hard that the rare shows that managed it are repeated on a loop basis. But at least with sitcom the runs are relatively short and the audience gets to draw breath between series. In Soap, the inveterate jester and/or the comic crackpot are with us several times a week for 52 weeks of the year, and that can become a literal turn-off if they are less than well written.

Taking comedy seriously

Producers may very well have to be persuaded, not to say press-ganged into taking the value of humour seriously, but as writers we need to promote its power and write it well enough to convince them. And to do that, writers must take the writing of humour seriously themselves. If humour isn't in your box of writers' tools, the set's lacking a valuable implement; and if you've just assumed that being funny isn't your forte, read up on it and try to learn some of the basic skills. (You could do worse than John Byrne's excellent *Writing Comedy*, published by A & C Black.)

I believe it's worth the effort because proper humour has substance enough to expose a character's strengths and insecurities, perhaps even more graphically than unrelenting tragedy ever could. Showing a character's foibles and fallibilities doesn't just make them entertaining – it makes them believable enough for the audience to identify with.

Seriously funny

Just as we need to take the business of writing comedy seriously, we need to remember that some of the funniest characters ever were not written as people who perceived themselves to be figures of fun. Basil Fawlty, Captain Mainwaring and Harold Steptoe, for example, were all drawn as people whose foibles were amusing to others. In Soap history, *Brookside*'s Harry Cross was a classic example of a character who took himself immensely seriously. Harry couldn't see the joke because he *was* the opinionated, truculent misanthrope. The writers trusted the audience to delight in his gloomy obstinacy, and they did.

An object lesson in current Soap terms is *Coronation Street*'s Fred Elliot. Fred the character does not set out to be a clown; it is, in fact, how seriously he takes himself that is so amusing.

Writing the opposite sex

Just as writers in any genre have to think themselves into characters who are unlike them in values and temperament, so they obviously have to be able to create characters of the opposite sex.

Broad strokes

There is a case for saying that writers often write best for their opposite gender, since we know our own all too well to imbue them with right for much, if any, of the time. But whether or not this is true, the biggest difficulty in maintaining any line of characterisation in Soap, be it male or female, is the perennial one that Soap too often tends – and is sometimes forced – to deal in broad strokes.

Where both male and female Soap characters are concerned, the off-screen ups-and-downs of Soap life – the loss of a cast-member causing a skew in plot, for example – can result in quite

aordinary personality transplants. Where the writer may well
e been able to manage subtle character developments in
response to altered circumstances in other forms of writing, Soap
can call for so sudden a lurch that both character and audience
are left reeling. Frankly, there isn't much the writer can do
about these unscheduled circumstances – except be aware that
the consequences for the characters can sometimes be quite
different depending on whether they are male or female.

'Saints and slags' – women soap characters

Where female characters are involved in any sudden character
lurch, the particular worry is that we still live in a society where
womens' sins – especially where sex and parenting are concerned – are less forgiveable than mens'. The Soap father who
suddenly ups and leaves his children, for instance, is unlikely to
become as reviled a character as the mother who deserts her
kids. A female Soap character endlessly swapping one relationship for another can be seen as a faithless hussy, whereas her
male counterpart can be sympathised with for not being able to
find the right woman. A promiscuous Soap man can be admired,
whereas their female equivalent may well be seen as the slag
whose exploits are only voyeuristically entertaining because
they are so abnormal and disgraceful. What's fascinating is how
often the largely female Soap audience judges the morals and
motives of female characters and finds them wanting.

To counterbalance this tendency to prejudice, writers can
only try to make the motivation of their female characters as
clear as possible whenever they get the chance and, most particularly, where sex, relationships and motherhood are concerned.
I'm not for a second advocating that honourable motives should
be ascribed to any and every Soap woman – a well-drawn
Medusa will do wonders for any drama. Rather that where plot
suddenly starts to dictate a different sort of behaviour, the female
character needs to be seen through it with a special awareness –
because however she falls from grace she will be so much
harder to redeem than a man.

You were wonderful, darling

Some recent research showed that much telling of lies goes on
between Soap characters, and that most of it is done by women.

I don't know if, in real life, we women do lie more than men. It's my experience that many females in a heterosexual relationship do, for instance, operate a system of telling their partner that everything cost exactly half of what it actually did; and certainly as the only sex that can fake orgasm, women have had more practice at (and perhaps more justification for) refining the art. On the other hand, it's often said that women, as opposed to men, generally choose to confront issues honestly and head-on rather than dissemble their way around any given issue. Whatever the reality of the generality, women in Soap do seem to be seen scheming and conniving their way through life and relationships more often than male characters.

The Saint Sheila syndrome

When, on the other hand, women are portrayed as good, they are frequently very-very good – sometimes bordering on too-good-to-be-true. The strong, selfless Earth Mother stereotype, for instance, is one that is often reinforced by Soap – a fact which may, ironically, be to do with the relatively small number of women writing them. I have certainly been on male-dominated teams where the men lean so far backwards to respect women, or to create their ideal ones, that there is no way to convince them that a female character could behave in a less than saintly way. I have to tell you it is supremely irking when you have been both a daughter and a mother to have some bloke – who obviously can have been neither – telling you how daughters *always* feel about their mothers.

Not that women on any particular writing team are always bound to agree about the emotions and motivations of a female character. We are sometimes as different from one another as we are from the opposite sex. A fact which was foreign to a script editor I once had who, having woken up to the reality that I was the only female writer on the team, interrupted my lunch-time pint with the lads to pat me sympathetically on the shoulder: 'Don't worry, Sweetie. We *will* be getting you another woman.' Years on, I'm still trying to come up with the right response to that one.

So if there is a case, which there sometimes is, for saying that women are badly drawn in Soap, it could be argued that it is because there are an awful lot of women characters in Soap

Operas but parity on writing teams is only just becoming a reality, and there are still fewer women than men producers.

It's a 'girl thang'

On the positive side, there is no doubt that Soap has addressed many hitherto unmentionable 'women's issues' and brought them into the public forum. Battered wives, breast cancer, rape, abortion and postnatal depression have been put on the popular dramatic agenda where they could only previously be aired in the most oblique and elitist ways. I deliberately left lesbianism out of this roll of honour because, unlike the portrayal of male homosexuality, Soap lesbianism thus far has only been allowable between the pretty – and, cynic that I am, something in me suspects that the motive may have as much to do with pandering to male fantasy as it does with fostering acceptance of a particular sexual orientation.

Men aren't from Venus

Of course, Soap men can also suffer from being drawn from a limited gallery of stereotypes. The handsome are more likely to be painted as Lotharios than looking for love, just as the short, fat funny-man often isn't allowed to have a rampant libido or a romantic bone in his chubby little body. It's a temptation when writing, as it is in life, to generalise traits under gender headings when, in actual fact, those characteristics are every bit as likely to manifest themselves in someone of our own sex. As a writer I know that I've sometimes been guilty of ascribing honourable motives to male characters for no better reason than that I would, ideally, like all men to have them – just as I have unfairly loaded unlovely characteristics on Soap men based on the lazy premise that *all* men are *like* that.

Writing with equality in mind

Be we male or female, perhaps the way writers can best serve both their own and the opposite sex is to strive always for equality of *character*. Ignoring gender to the point of not making assumptions as to how it would make the character behave, and seeing them simply as a personality with their own unique set of reactions, will inevitably make for more interesting and less stereotyped individuals.

It's an exercise worth the effort, since tramlining our characters by sex doesn't just run the risk of creating a gallery of simplistically drawn protagonists, it inevitably dictates and restricts the routes down which they can travel in story terms. By unhitching characters from their perceived – and often erroneous – gender yokes and portraying them instead as having diverse human, rather than specific male/female agendas, Soap stories stand more chance of escaping the narrow confines of cliché.

So what if it is a man's world?

If writers can successfully compose characters of the opposite sex, it could be argued that it doesn't matter that Soap is still something of a male preserve. On the other hand, it could be said that having an equal number of both sexes on board is the only way to create a true balance, because even where writers can avoid sexual stereotyping of their opposite gender they can never represent the actual experience of *being* male or female. And it is experience that creates and colours perspective, dictates priorities and explains motivations. Just as a phalanx of women writers creating male characters would stand to overlook some fundamental ingredient of masculinity, so an overwhelmingly male team risks having some crucial blind spots.

Since the latter is by far the likeliest scenario, I think it's fair to hope that, as more women become powerful among the ranks of programme-providers and more the norm in production and direction, they will foster more women writers – not as an act of positive discrimination but on merits that will redress the idosyncratic situation where men are still overwhelmingly responsible for creating popular drama for a predominently female Soap audience.

6. Really Nearly Real

When people tell you in that wouldn't-be-caught-dead voice that they never watch the Soap you write for, they often go on to explain that this is because they think the storylines – all of which they appear to be minutely conversant with – are too far-fetched. Declared devotees often level the same criticism along the lines of, 'I'm not saying I don't enjoy it, but. . . Well, let's face it, isn't like *my* life.' It's hard not to snap that it wouldn't be, would it? Since, from what they have told you, the highlight of their life is a double de-caff cocoa just before the watershed strikes. What they all mean is that drama isn't like real life. And the only answer to that is: Well, no, it isn't.

Even documentaries aren't real as such in that they are slivers of life seen through someone else's eyes and even that second-hand experience is then edited. Only real life is real life. Fiction – however close it comes to an experience we have had, or however close it brings us to experiencing something that hasn't happened to us – is still fiction. It has a shape which real life rarely has. And it cannot be boring, which real life all too often is.

It's a long story

The value of coinciding on-screen stories with annual seasonal events as they are happening to the audience in real life has already been covered (*see* Chapter 2, pp. 27–9). This section is mainly dedicated to story timing in a different sense, that is to say the *duration* of happenings in Soap life as opposed to how long they would take in the real world. These happenings may be the sort that have a quantifiable timescale, give or take a week or so here and there – for example, matters such as pregnancy, school-term lengths and the time it takes a solicitor to sort out the conveyancing on a house (!). Or they may be the sort of instances for which there is no definite schedule – recovery from illness, periods of mourning, etc.

Just how closely Soap stories should mimic the timescale of reality is an interesting and perpetual quandary. On the one hand, the similarities that viewers can draw between their own lives and those of their favoured Soap's characters is one of the genre's great pulling powers; on the other hand, what that same audience wants is diverting drama of which one of the key elements is variety. If a note, even a recognisable one, is held too long it becomes monotonous. The dilemma for Soap writers is how long is too long.

Life can be tedious, drama daren't risk it

I was once involved in a piece of planning where the Producer and writers became committed to the idea of running a storyline about unemployment in real time. That is to say we would resist having the character out of work just long enough for us to wreak the dramatic value. Determined to make a proper job of reflecting a widespread social evil of the time, we agreed we wouldn't gallop our character through the gamut from initial optimism to the edge of despair and then neatly find him another job. The reality for a man of our character's age was that he would never work again.

Having taken our time and given what we thought was due weight to his bullish early attempts to find work, his catalogue of soul-crunching disappointments, his rage and eventual feelings of uselessness, we were left with the most acute reality of all. For a middle-aged man of such limited resources, real life was remorselessly empty and mind-numbingly boring. Troopers that we were, both writers and actor persevered in an attempt to make precisely that painful point, even though finding ways of showing the character doing nothing were as taxing to write as they were to act. The fall-out from his mental and physical inertia as it affected – and disaffected – those around him was, of course, part of what we wanted to show and gave us drama that was easier to illustrate. But it was peripheral to the central dilemma as experienced by the man himself, which was that he had nothing to do.

The audience wearied of it before we did. Viewing figures fell and enough letters registering catatonic boredom fell onto the production office mat to convince us that we were on a hiding to nothing. We resorted to the unlikely and found our character a job.

A similar thing happened with a postnatal depression story some while later. In order to show as graphically as possible that the miserable condition was no respecter of persons, the storyline was played with one of the characters who was loved for her vibrancy and indefatigable ability to cope. At first the bouquets came thick and fast – columns of critical acclaim at the way a Cinderella subject was being aired and handled; grateful letters from women who were having or had had the problem themselves. Again the intention had been not to undermine the seriousness of the topic by taking it too fast. Before very long, though, viewers started to complain that the character had become boring and whinging to the verge of unwatchable. By popular request, the character recovered before it was likely that any real-life counterpart would.

Maybe in both of these cases (as in others where I've seen the same thing happen) we simply didn't do it well enough to sustain the audience's interest. Maybe we did it too well and all too graphically recreated aspects of the very reality that some of our viewers were watching television in order to escape.

Time flies when you're having fun

But only up to a point. Even where more lighthearted topics are concerned, it is difficult to predetermine the point at which a Soap story will stop being captivating and start tasting stale to an audience. Perhaps the more fundamental reason for the failure of these real-time excursions is that, as an audience, we are more used to the unnaturalistic pace of Soap than we realise. Time is so often telescoped in ways we either don't notice or are prepared to accept in order to maintain the momentum of a story. The length of time it takes for the legal process to bring a person to trial, say, or the time it would take to obtain any sort of licence, buy property, get results of medical tests and so on, is frequently chibbled down to something shorter than it would be in reality. So often that a tale played out in real time can seem excruciatingly slow.

All the writer can do to forestall the unpredictable point at which the magic turns to monotony is to make certain that they find as many variations within the theme as they can. Where characters' reactions are concerned, the Soap writer needs to move as often as possible away from cliché to create and explore novel slants on well-worn themes.

Why so much happens to so few

Another criticism that gets levelled at Soap surrounds just how much happens to so few people in so short a time. In most viewers' lives it is fairly rare for such a rapid succession of things to happen to an individual. Seeing so much happen to a screen character is, therefore, bound to separate Soap from the audience's experience of reality. It's a valid point and, in the past, I have been known to argue on the side of the critics about this one. The situation arises, of course, out of there only ever being a set gallery of characters through which to tell an endless succession of stories. To counteract it, maybe there should be a bigger through-put of characters, any or all of whom would move off at given natural points just as people in real life do. That way, we wouldn't have what usually ends up being a preposterous number of events happening to one character. On top of which it would leave the writers with fewer credibility gaps to bridge. You know the sort of thing – Desmond couldn't get his just desserts for what he'd done to Dolores' cat because he can't be lost from the cast so, somehow, he has to be reconstituted to the point where the audience believe he'll make a wonderful vet. It would also go some way towards dealing with the incestuous nature of Soap wherein, sooner or later, everybody ends up having relationships with everybody else.

After all, it's hard enough to be convincing about why the most unlikely people end up living together in the non-sexual sense – which is, incidentally, because most budgets won't stretch to many, if any, single-occupancy sets. In the same way, because the money is too limited to run to many workplace settings, characters tend to come home at all sorts of unlikely times. And have you ever noticed how characters in television Soaps virtually never watch television and seldom, if ever, talk about it? That's not just because it would be pretty boring to watch someone watching the telly, it's because most shows don't want to pay to show glimpses of other people's programmes. And many Soap characters are seemingly oblivious to the joys of music for the same budgetary reasons. On one show I worked on, the only music we were allowed to use was that produced by a tame composer who was adept at creating sound alikes of everything from Lennon to Liszt. Characters couldn't even sing 'Happy Birthday' to each other because the song is still in copyright.

At least some character-gallery flexibility, it seemed to me, would redress the balance of these non-realities a bit; equal more believability all round. In the end, though, I became convinced that it was a great deal easier said than done.

One of the great pulling powers of Soap is that the audience comes to know and love (or to love to hate) the central core of characters. With very few exceptions, new characters need nestling into the audience's affections before the viewers can be expected to care what happens to them. In other words, before they can carry a central story. Those rare creatures who don't require this running-in are seized upon and given so much to do so fast that their feet don't touch the ground long enough for them to consider toddling off to do theatre or a rival Soap.

But these captivating creatures apart, ongoing cast turnover would mean having to spend time on establishing an endless succession of characters which, of course, would mean that much less room for stories. And since there is already an ongoing element of natural wastage in any cast – wastage that can happen at the drop of a hat, dropping the story plans right in it – it would be folly to add to it. At the end of the day, the traditional Soap format of establishing a stable gallery of characters and foreshortening the sequence of events that happen to them exists because, on the whole, it works.

For the writer there is no point in railing against the size of cast or canvas Soap can offer. Think of them as limitations and the writing will invariably point them up as just that; embrace them as challenging idiosyncrasies of the genre and there is much more chance of creating something convincing. Motivate the character well enough in whatever bizarre direction Soap's lego-logic dictates, and you will take the audience with them.

Audience sensibilities

How graphic a representation of reality the audience wants within those unrealistic parameters is another matter altogether.

Often, the very same viewers who carp loudest about Soap being a sentimentalised cipher are the first to balk at being shown too convincing a picture of actuality. Even though, sans censorship, sans small-mindedness, sans squeamishness, sans everything, that is all it can ever be – a representation of the real – they are, nonetheless, afraid of it. Why, when we're back to the second-hand experience of drama, which can never be anywhere near as brutal, random, horrific and flagrantly cruel as reality, they are afraid is an even more complicated question. And I'm not at all sure I can answer it.

The difficulty in pinning down exactly what any given audience will find offensive, outrageous, distasteful or downright unbearable, is that they are not an entity but a collection of individual sensitivities. A Soap may be crossing the line with a section of its viewers in one scene while the rest of the audience may be finding it manageably uncomfortable and compelling viewing. In the scene that follows, this profile may be instantly reversed for a whole or a part of the selfsame audience, making it hard for programme-makers to decide how much validity should be given to any or all of these ever-shifting levels of tolerance.

Where they are left in absolutely no doubt at all is where too many sensibilities have been upset by the same thing at the same time, precipitating avalanches of viewer complaints and howls of censure from television watchdogs. At this point I ought to say that, in my experience, nervous programme-makers of all dispositions can read an 'avalanche' into anything from a half-dozen to half-a-hundred protests out of an audience of millions, and are all too ready to run scared of even the most toothless of watchdogs. Since there is no second-guessing specific tolerance levels, the Soap writer can only bring their own value judgements to bear as to what is valid and not gratuitous – and be prepared to be taken by surprise by what upsets whom.

Seeing things

On the subject of outrage, though, there is an odd phenonemon whereby viewers have been known to complain about something they only imagined they saw or heard. In one graphic instance, a storyline about incest brought forth a flurry of folk outraged at us having shown a father in bed with his daughter. Response to the moral indignation in this case was simple and, I have to admit, almost perversely satisfying: we *didn't* show the father in bed with his daughter.

What we had shown was the father in bed and an older daughter at the doorway looking in. From her expression we deduced that her younger sister was also in the bed. The more florid picture of father and daughter in bed together came entirely from the minds of those who had complained about the disgraceful image they had seen.

The same show was sometimes the subject of unexplained sightings in a more general sense. Perceived to be overly violent, the strict policy during all the years I worked on it was that no physical blow could ever be seen to land.

The good news for the writer in these examples is that they never need feel hamstrung by censorship or watersheds when the plotline merits something powerful, explicit or disturbing. With skilful writing and stage direction the writer can legitimately manoeuvre their audience towards the graphic and stop just short of it in the sure and certain knowledge that the camera of the mind will keep running.

With only a shadow and shower curtain, Hitchcock left one of the most memorable screen images etched on the minds of millions, just as other artful film-makers have shown us everything from Satan to steamy sex in scenes that we never actually saw.

'Bad' language

On the same show discussed above, bad language was forever manifesting itself in the minds of members of the audience. True, the show had begun its life using a smattering of mild swear-words, but having been shown the yellow card by the channel that bought it while suffering a simultaneous drop in audience figures, the ruling on expletives had gone out very early on. They would always be deleted. And, again, in my own long experience of the show, they always were.

Many a writer, including myself, made impassioned pleas for what we argued would be the realistic use of the odd 'bloody' in some character's dialogue – with, ironically, much stronger language being used to debate the very point – but for all the effing and blinding I can't remember a single one of us getting so much as a playground profanity onto the screen. What a section of the audience often perceived as a foul-mouthed brawl was often, from the writer's point of view, a preposterously polite exchange.

To this day there is virtually no cussing in British Soaps, certainly no four-letter words and absolutely no blasphemy. Not even the toughest, roughest and most ill-fated of *East-Enders* is allowed to say, 'Oh God.' From the writer's point of view this restriction on vocabulary can be frustrating. The more acutely trained the writer's ear is to real-life everyday exchanges, the more aware they are of how much 'bad' language is woven into so much of it. Ignoring the existence of those who preface and litter every utterance with profanity is often less of a hardship for the writer, since (unless illustrating poverty of language is the whole point) it can be tedious to write and wearing to listen to. Its biggest drawback for the Soap writer, though, is that this endlessly repetitious graffiti-speak can take a long time to move through – or come to – any point. It's more of a loss when the writer knows that a particular characterisation is incomplete without access to the odd curse, or where a normally clean-spoken character is robbed of resorting to vivid language *in extremis*. In either case, substituting a coy alternative seldom achieves the same effect. What it will do is point up the missing expletive and make the character seem ludicrously prim when what you were going for was something altogether more powerful.

It's far safer to signify strength of feeling and/or intensity of reaction with some well-turned sarcasm, an increase in volume, a short, cutting remark or an angry gesture. Do it well enough and your audience will believe that the air was every bit as blue as you would have liked.

Who sets the agenda?

Although many of these restraints and constraints are to do with the fact that most Soaps appear before the nine o'clock watershed, there is also undoubtedly an element of self-censorship by producers. Given the fluctuating feast that has always been the audience's pain threshold, plus the end-of-civilisation-as-we-know-it outcry that has so often been the consequence of getting too close to reality, it's hardly surprising that the increasing tendency among Soap producers has been for playing it on the safe side.

But if there is an answer to why it is getting harder rather than easier to portray reality, warts and all, audience squeamishness and hands still stinging from being smacked may not be the whole of it. It could have at least something to do with where television executives, producers, directors, storyliners, editors and, ultimately, writers are demographically drawn from. Where it is increasingly from the middle-class, media-graduate pool it can come as no surprise that shows veer less often from the middle of the road. By the same token, a creative team that sees nothing above or beyond the working class as being worthy of depiction is likely to offer as narrow a perspective.

Agendas set entirely by the like-minded are limited. Apart from the tendency to stay safely within a set of sanitised parameters, there is a danger that any forum representing only one stratum will *mis*represent anything above as well as below its own social register. It's easy to spot where this has been the case when a Soap character, or sometimes an entire family, hasn't been imported in a genuine attempt to enrich the mix but merely to serve as a grotesque foil for the show's more seriously regarded 'norm'.

Since the writer has no control over the programme's creative social mix, they can only be on the lookout for any imbalance and counter it wherever possible through their own contribution. At the storylining stage, making a case for putting equal meat on the bones of *all* the characters, as well as urging the avoidance of class cliché storylines, may occasionally work. If it doesn't, the writer can only try to redress the balance by giving one-dimensional characters some extra thought at the writing stage – looking for any and every opportunity to slip in the odd subtle glimpse of a facet that will rescue the character from the shallows. Looking up or down at another man's lot, rather than being in a position to reflect it from something closer to first-hand experience, doesn't, of course, mean that you can't portray it. To do it properly, though, a writer needs to respect the raw material they utilise, no matter where it is drawn from. Otherwise their characters can seem more hologram than human, and the depiction of their lives can feel more like a voyeuristic foray than a genuine exploration.

Facts – well, close enough

Never let the facts get in the way of a good story. Sensible advice when it's levelled at a Soap writer who insists on plodding too pedantically through the actual and factual machinations of a particular plot. And, no, we're not talking here about the same thing as in the last section: this is not about the fundamental paths of truth from which good Soap never really needs to deviate if it's done properly. The subject here isn't the motive or the moral imperative behind a storyline, but the mechanics.

As touched on earlier, the drive that needs to be maintained in any Soap sometimes calls for a foreshortening of the timing of events. In life we must languish helplessly 'on hold' while we wait for hospital test results, judicial hearings, a promotion, the sack, and all manner of happenings. In Soap, we can't. At least not without risking the audience forgetting or ceasing to care about what was being waited for. But however unrealistically soon Soap events occur, they do need to bear more than a passing resemblance to reality when they appear on screen.

Research

With their own novel or a play, a writer would set their own timescale for doing all the background research they needed. However, the Soap writer's schedule doesn't allow for such a luxury, which is why – in most cases – research is gathered, collated and condensed into more easily digestible bite-sizes by someone other than the writer.

Where there isn't a person with the specific job designation of Researcher within the Soap organisation, a writer will often be supplied with a selection of experts whose brains they can pick first-hand. As well as these tame advisors on subjects such as the law or medicine, the Researcher (or someone on the production team) may also, from time to time, arrange for the writer to have access to people in a particular field of work or someone who has direct experience of a particular situation. On some shows the writer is offered the whole shebang – the good offices of a researcher who will supply relevant information, access to expert advisors *and* the opportunity to talk to sundry individuals. However the background information is delivered or sought, there is always a danger of there being more of it than the writer needs to know, which is where one element of not letting the facts get in the way of a good story comes in.

Paralysis by analysis

A conscientious researcher can end up producing a small library of articles, facts, figures and assorted info on any given topic. A zealous expert advisor can provide more working practice and case histories than could be digested in a month of Sundays. Take the two in tandem and the writer could end up with a well-intended avalanche from which they must snatch only those flakes of information closest in bearing to the specific storyline. It's not unknown for panic and paralysis to set in as to where one starts when deluged by this embarrassment of riches.

It can be frustrating to have so much interesting and valid material to hand when the tight strictures governing the space allowed for any one story-strand rarely allow for anywhere near all of it to be utilised. And frustration hardly covers it when, as sometimes happens, research, case studies or first-hand experiences turn up a much better story than the one the writer has been charged with executing.

Staying on course

Every now and again it may be possible to get the show's Producer to see the merits of veering off onto this different and better tack but, for the most part, this kind of deviation from the originally planned storyline isn't an option. As you'll have gathered by now, by the writing stage it's already late in the day for much, if any, reweaving of a major story-strand that may not only involve the rescheduling of actors and call for sets or locations other than planned, but necessitate the unravelling of several surrounding plotlines. More usually, the writer must select a small ration from the tomes of research on offer with which to add texture to the storyline they've already got.

Save it for the book

Any fascinating detail surplus to Soap requirements just has to be left aside in the hopes that there'll be a chance to explore and air it another day. The more complete and complex glimpse you've been given of some issue or other may one day add depth to a play or a film or a book. For now, the brief for the writer being paid to write Soap is to distil the possibilities down to an essence. Something informed enough and sound enough around which to create convincing drama; to make it feel real within the remit.

'There may always be another reality to make fiction of the truth we think we've arrived at.'   (Christopher Fry)

Too right. Even the real 'real' isn't always guaranteed to convince. This I can testify to, having once worked on a storyline involving a character who was deaf. In an attempt to handle the theme responsibly, extensive and thorough research was done into the issues and into day-to-day experiences faced by people with profound hearing difficulties. With an actress who was herself deaf being hired to play the part, we could hardly get closer to being convincing.

Wrong.

How, demanded one particularly exasperated viewer, had we managed to portray a deaf person so inaccurately? Why, for goodness sake, hadn't we used a real deaf person? As the mother of a daughter who was deaf the woman knew whereof she spake and, according to her, our character was nowhere near real. Hard to know how to respond, really. What the viewer meant was that the character wasn't like *her* deaf daughter. And, well, no, she probably wasn't. No more was the painstakingly researched cancer story a straight reflection of every individual cancer victim's trauma, or the Alzheimer saga a replay of each and every relative's experience in dealing with it.

These are illustrations, I suppose, that do straddle both this section and the last when it comes to credibility. Drama can come close to someone's truth, but never everyone's. And a story based on all the facts, figures, research and background information in the world will leave someone, somewhere, unconvinced. With the best will in the world there are, of course, times when things slip through the net. And then there are times when storyline subjects are shabbily researched, lazily written or just plain wrong. When it happens – whether it be by genuine accident or sloppy practice – there's no use pretending nobody will notice. They will.

Tackling tough subjects

When there is an abundance of the right research, and the writer wades nobly through it, it can be an illuminating exercise and a chance to do wonders for your general understanding, not to mention your general knowledge. There are times, though, when it can be a depressing and distressing experience.

Graphic descriptions of child abuse, for one unlovely instance, together with reams of statistics showing how shamingly prevalent it is, do not make for comfortable reading. If, however, you have agreed to write the storyline – maybe have even been complicit in devising it – the onus for sifting through the unsavoury realities rests, fairly and squarely, on your shoulders. The more disturbing the issue, the more the writer needs to know about it – if, that is, they care about creating a meaningful depiction.

Not letting the facts get in the way of a good story is one thing when it comes to the lighter side of Soap life: it is, in fact, what the writer's paid to do – to bend actuality, sidestep tedious detail and tinker with amorphous timescales in order to create well-paced entertainment. Where the responsibility gets to weigh more heavily is when a Soap that trumpets its own dedication to realism strays onto the more serious side of the life we're told it depicts. Then, if too much is skewed, disregarded and distorted for expediency's sake, what might have been worthwhile drama can end up looking like gratuitous dross.

Where research won't help

Where research, good, bad or indifferent, can be the least help is where much of the stuff of Soaps lies – in relationships. For feelings, the writer has to rely on what teams of experts and statistics can never supply them with: raw experience. And, where that experience is absent, an innate ability to empathise.

Soap history is sacrosanct

It always pays to stick strictly to the facts when they have been created by the Soap itself. For instance, if the fact of a Soap character's life is that he is a vegetarian, the writer cannot have him calling in for a kebab on his way home from the pub.

In an effort to stop writers falling too frequently into this kind of trap, there is often some form of bible available to them. In the best-organised Soaps, this collection of biographies of all the major characters – their predilictions, politics and history – is regularly updated by an archivist. Individual character outlines may well have begun with the orginal invention of the character, and can be as specific as defining what newspaper he or she reads; what car they drive; how many, if any, brothers and sisters they have; which way they vote; and all manner of mores and minutiae that describe their make-up.

On other shows there is no specific archivist and no actual documentation – just someone whom everyone else hopes will never get knocked down because they *are* the bible. These precious people possess an elephantine ability to carry in their heads every single thing that has ever happened to every character since the show began, along with a comprehensive catalogue of each character's likes and dislikes, aspirations and allergies.

However this information is available to the writer, it is sensible not to argue with it. Even if the Producer would let you get away with Desmond the devout Methodist nipping out to Confession, an astonishing number of the audience wouldn't.

Many Happy Returns!

On most shows the writers will be reminded at the story-planning stage of any red-letter days in the characters' lives, such as birthdays and anniversaries. The acknowledgement of these milestones helps to maintain a sense of character reality, and the occasions in themselves can offer story potential. On a contained scale within a particular relationship, the birthday hubby who forgets or pretends to forget when he has, in fact, planned a surprise party, or the wedding anniversary celebration that turns the spotlight onto a failing marriage, are all grist to the Soap writer's mill.

On a wider-ranging scale these celebration times also provide that comparatively rare Soap scenario where it seems entirely natural for characters of different families, types and backgrounds to be assembled under the same roof. Such gatherings then become an unmissable opportunity for the passions and politics between characters to merge, surface or change in nature for better or for worse. A character's birthday party, for instance, can have widespread story ramifications: who gets invited or not may revive old feuds or create new ones; uninvited spectres at the feast may wind up the ante on some already ongoing strand; new alliances may be formed or warring parties reconciled.

You can't say that!

One of the other responsibilities a researcher or research department may have is to check that the writer doesn't accidentally or deliberately infringe any libel laws. Defamation of a real-life person or organisation can lead to an action for damages or, at the very least, send injured parties scuttling to one of the regulatory bodies demanding a broadcast retraction and apology. Naturally no producer wants to spend time and money on defending legal action, or suffer the ignominy of having to admit that their Soap said something it shouldn't, so the writer needs to exercise extreme caution when referring specifically to the real world.

Character dialogue that mentions real people (particularly politicians and anyone with celebrity status) in an insulting way or that implies corruption or criminality will not survive, so there is no point in the writer creating it. By the same token, a speech that attacks a specific company's corporate values or products will not be acceptable – no matter how good a case the writer thinks they have for wanting their character to air the view. And from personal experience I can tell you that saying something derogatory about a real restaurant, no matter how bad a meal you had there, can get you and your Soap into deep trouble – so there's no way you'll be allowed to wreak your revenge that way.

To guard against the writer *inadvertently* giving a real name to a fictitious firm or business, there will most probably be a 'negative check' made by someone in the programme's research department. If there proves to be a real firm of solicitors registered in the name of Baffle, Waffle & Fleece, the writer will be asked to invent an alternative.

Whoops!

However careful the writer or researchers are to avoid giving cause for complaint or offence, it has been known to come about quite accidently. In one instance some years ago, a haulage-firm owner was happy to hire out some of his vehicles for a Soap scene. Unfortunately no-one thought to change the company name on the rigs, and the owner was less than delighted that what an audience of millions saw was *his* firm's wagons breaking through picket lines at a time when real-life disputes were rife.

7. On the Hook

The Hook, the cliff-hanger, the tantalising carrot that keeps them coming back for more was around before serial drama was so much as a gleam in a soap sponsor's eye. Sensationally suspenseful or subtly buried, hooks have forever been employed in all forms of fiction and drama to sustain the narrative drive. Where Soap is concerned, the purpose of the device is the same – to have the audience wanting to know what happens next.

Propellers

The hook device is also used as integrally and organically in Soap as it is with the novel or play in that, within the broad scheme of dramatic thrust, there are smaller 'propellers' employed to draw the audience's interest along. In Soap terms this means managing to engage the audience with a series of ongoing issues that regular characters are dealing with, while keeping the pot boiling fast and furiously on currently major storylines. Just as in the novel or play, these background and forefront story-strands are ideally designed to reach peaks in their different levels of development at well-paced points throughout the piece.

The never-ending story

The difference lies, of course, in where this mesh of minor and major impetus is driving towards. In the play or novel the destination is a resolution of the whole: one final dénouement. Done well, a satisfactory culmination for author and audience alike. Soap, on the other hand, has no closing chapter or final act. Each episode somehow has to stand as a fulfilling experience, complete in itself, while always leaving strands unresolved so that they can be picked up and run with into what amounts, in writing terms, to eternity. Hopefully taking the audience with them.

That Soap never reaches a point of closure (unless it's axed) would seem to be one of the prime reasons for putting characterisation first and story second. That the fashion on some Soaps has altered in favour of doing the reverse can only represent a death-wish.

Caring who's hanging from the cliff

As an audience for any writing, we all know that the most dynamic plot in the world will leave us cold if we do not care about the characters moving through it. We do not necessarily need to like the character(s), but we do need to be able to connect with some human aspects of them if we're to be properly interested in their fate. Where we do believe in a character, where we have been carefully and consistently brought to care about and identify with their lot, it is valid for us to be taken with them through their various ups and downs. It is just as valid, though, for us to feel manipulated and cheated when we have been dragged through the emotional mill for some chimera of a character whose motivations shift simply to accommodate every passing storyline.

The danger of the Producer and writers falling for the easy option of bending any one particular character's personality around a story, instead of the other way about, is that the rot tends to spread with alarming speed. Next thing you know, every character in the show is down with a bad case of credibility-deficit – ending in the *reductio ad absurdum* of having sacrificed characterisation to story so often that there is no-one convincing enough left to carry the show into the next story. From there on in there is only spiralling ever faster from one stratospheric improbability to the next. Such short-sightedness is stunning – and ultimately suicidal.

Hooks, hooks and more hooks

With so many Soaps competing for viewer loyalty, 'The Hook' aspect of the storytelling has become even more crucial. Even within a particular Soap, the increase in episode output means that the writing team may be faced with having to devise several end-of-episode hooks in any one week. Even if plotting is done by storyliners and the hooks handed down, it falls to the writer to make them work. The number of hooks multiplies, of course, if the show goes out on a commercial channel, because each episode will need a halfway hook designed to entice viewers back after the ad-break.

Each and every scene ending should provide a form of hook in itself (*see* also pp. 110–11), in the sense that it leaves the audience curious or interested enough to want to follow developments through the rest of the episode. However, it is the end-of-part and, even more critically, the end-of-episode punctuations that Soap relies so heavily upon for its ongoing survival.

Making hooks work

Given that hooks are, by definition, the point at which emotion and suspense reach their highest pitch, it's not easy to stop them looking ludicrously melodramatic on screen. Hooks are, if you like, where the contrivance of Soap shows up most obviously and where the writing needs to be at its cleverest. With an audience exposed to so much Soap that the mechanisms are no longer a mystery to them, it gets ever harder to invent hooks that will be successfully subliminal and/or unpredictable.

That isn't to say that a certain degree of hook-planning doesn't rely on that very familiarity. As with the fairy story or the novel we know off by heart, there's comfortable enjoyment to be had out of there being no real surprises – just as, on first reading, there's a certain amount of satisfaction in being able to second-guess some element of plot or character reaction. In the following extract by Simon Frith for *The Archers*, the writer not only knows his Joe character but also knows how well the audience knows him.

CLARRIE: Oh and Joe. It's Friday. Where are those tickets?
JOE: (BEAT) Come on, Clarrie, I only just got out of bed!
CLARRIE: When will I have them back?
JOE: You had my word. Friday I said, and Friday it's gonna be!

The stage direction of a beat before Joe answers is the only concrete hint that there may be upcoming twists and turns in the ticket story. For the rest, the writer relies on established characterisation to offer the audience the tantalising possibility that, despite Joe's protestations, he may not be able to deliver.

Surprise, surprise

Of course, if the writers rely too often on the technique of letting a character's predictability carry the hook, it will lose its potency. The trick is in being able to offset the familiarity factor with enough departures to stop it turning into contempt. One way of injecting novelty is to play deliberately on the audience's assumptions as to what a hook will be and divert it into something different at the last second. Another is to double-bluff by inveigling the audience into thinking they have seen beyond the obvious and can second-guess the hook – and then to do something completely different from that.

Well executed and used sparingly, these sorts of devices can stop the audience – and the writers – becoming complacent about the way a particular story or character is going and have a generally refreshing effect on the show as a whole. Used clumsily and too often they can confuse and infuriate an audience to the point of complete, and literal, turn-off.

False hooks

Something else that doesn't – and shouldn't – work is the false hook. This is where the writers and/or storyliners have let all the themes sail into the doldrums in the same episode and panic into inventing some spurious cliffhanger. Not having had any real reason for existence in the first place, these bogus bombshells have nothing to do but fizzle dismally out at the front of the next episode or, even worse, be forgotten altogether.

Too much titillation of this type for what turns out to be no valid reason, and the frustrated audience stops believing that they'll ever get satisfaction. And, once they stop trusting their excitement, interest and concern to the writers, the whole point of the hook is negated.

All cliffhangers great and small

As Soap consumers, we can probably all call to mind a couple of the Big Hooks. Raise a rheumatic hand all those Home Service Soap-saga-louts who weren't on the edge of their seat the night the flames crackled over the airwaves threatening to annihilate the fragrant Grace Archer. Which they did, of course, in what was probably the first piece of cynical programming used in this country. That this opening volley of engineering a revered character's death (with the specific aim of diverting attention away from ITV's debut) started a scheduling war the Beeb have been bemoaning ever since is interesting – and not beside the point when it comes to demonstrating the power that hooks have long been perceived to have.

Will the innocent Deidre be sent to jail? Are Sue and the baby dead? Is the breast cancer back? Will Barry shoot the dog? (!) (Astonishingly – or perhaps not in this animal-besotted nation of ours – among the harrowing human tenterhooks that audiences have been placed on, a character threatening to kill a dog elicited one of the most outraged responses I've ever come across.) But the real point is, these are all mega-moments and even the most sensation-driven Soaps need a regular and ongoing supply of everyday emotional precipices upon which the characters – and with them, the audience – are left standing.

Scene hooks

Having already established that every scene should have one, scene hooks can sometimes encompass different elements from those needed for the end-of-part or end-of-episode. One of these elements is defined by the Editor of *The Archers* as 'The Ahh Hook'. Whereas it would be dangerous to let the audience come out of an episode on a note of resolution, an end-of-scene can sometimes be allowed to offer more satisfaction than suspense. A cuddle of reconciliation, say, or a rare meeting of minds between traditional antagonists would not fit the bill when it came to leaving the audience on tenterhooks, but done well, such moments can provide the occasional welcome feeling of fulfilment. They can also punctuate what, otherwise, can seem like a relentless agenda of unfinished business.

110

This being Soap, however, the very best of these small moments of satisfaction will always manage to have a stray strand buried within them; a subliminal thread left hanging to create a sense that this may not, after all, be the end of the story.

Building to the hook

Whether it be a scene, end-of-part or end-of-episode hook, the writer needs to judge the speed of build towards it. Pitching any scene on too high an emotional level from the outset gives the actor(s) nowhere to go in terms of performance and can make for exhausting viewing. In the same way, scene after scene of relentlessly high-octane drama can leave the episode with nowhere to go and the audience too spent to care. It may help to picture the episode as a succession of inclines up which you must draw the viewer – the lower slopes being the scenes and the episode hook being the summit. Since a breakneck assault risks leaving casualties along the way, it's obviously sensible to set a steadier pace interspersed with incentives and the odd reward. Engender enough interest and curiosity to keep them climbing and, beyond a certain point of investment, the audience will be positively raring to scale that final face. *Then* when you leave them hanging a foot from the clifftop you really do have a hook. And, since it's one the audience were made to feel increasingly complicit in reaching, they're more likely to enjoy, rather than resent, being suspended.

The final cut

What occasionally does blight even the most properly devised and competently composed of hooks is something that is out of the writer's hands. It's where, again, the punishing schedule of Soap production can have its pitfalls.

All it takes to turn a hook from engrossing tension to titter-inducing is an actor's under-rehearsed and over-theatrical expression – or a directorial decision to hold shot on an appropriate expression long enough for it to start looking silly. Those last crucial seconds are notoriously difficult to write, perform and time to perfection. That we are, as an audience, more often left gripped than groaning is another testimony to the skills involved.

It isn't necessary to pretend that hooks aren't a way of pulling an audience's strings, since art of all kinds does just that. As in all things, what separates the valuable stuff from the dross is how well it's done.

8. No, I Liked It. I Did. It's Just...

... that he didn't like it all. Your favourite line out of the whole script, probably out of your entire writing career, has just bitten the dust. And it hurts.

The thing that producers and script editors never seem to understand – and yet strangely all writers do – is that when he or she says, 'Don't you think it would be better if. . . ?', you don't. Not ever. Not really. Otherwise you would have written it that way in the first place. If they've any sense a writer may be persuaded to see the merits of an alternative way of saying something, or they may feel it's politic to fake it while knowing, deep down in some nether corner of their soul, that their way would have worked as well – if not better. That sounds arrogant, and it is; but seeing as how being a writer calls for a kind of conceit, it's hard to avoid. If authors of any ilk didn't believe they had a gift for observing and serving life back up in the dramatic shapes of novels, plays or whatever, they would confine themselves to penning postcards. It also takes bottle to dredge up bits of you; to borrow fragments of your own painful experience and personality, and bare them to the world through what you write.

That, in essence, is why first-draft meetings – known in writers' minds as rewrite meetings – can be a depressing experience. Sometimes in a small way, sometimes in a large, for sure something of the carefully crafted offering of this bit of self will be chibbled away or brutally hacked off.

Rewrites are a reality

Fair or not, the fact that Soap writing will call for rewrites is an immutable fact. The only thing a writer can change is their own attitude to having to do them. On a show such as *Eastenders*, for example, where a writer may be asked to produce anything up to five or six drafts of their script before it is finally deemed acceptable, flexibility is obviously a key requirement for the job. No matter how many drafts are the norm, though, a Soap writer has to see the aim of any cutting and rewriting as a way of reducing the episode to its pure essence, and co-operate in working towards that end.

The first-draft meeting

Depending on the Soap, and how many draft stages are allowed, there may not be any face-to-face draft meeting as such, but rather a discussion – or series of discussions – conducted by phone, fax or email during which alterations and refinements are outlined. Or, there may be a series of face-to-face meetings designed to distil the episode(s) down to what the Producer wants.

On other Soaps, especially some of those where the second draft is expected to be the definitive one, an actual first draft meeting is convened. These meetings usually come after a week or so during which time the Script Editor and Producer will have read all the scripts in the block. Time during which the writer can exercise their creative inventiveness to the full by imagining the only first-draft meeting in history where the Producer simply sighs happily and pronounces the script perfect.

In reality, the writer will have either a relatively painless or an absolutely agonising ordeal to face. Whether they are invited to face the music alone or alongside the other writers in that block of episodes depends on the show's set-up. The rationale for calling all the writers involved in a block to come together and have their work tinkered with – or torn apart – in front of each other is that whatever one writer has to alter in or about their script will affect the rest of the writers in the room. It makes sense. But there are times when having scripts marked in public takes you right back to the quandary of schoolroom survival. While the best part of you writhes, an unlovely atom relishes watching someone else getting told they've got it wrong.

And should the writer in the hot-seat protest, you have only a couple of similarly queasy options. One is to side with them – meaning against the Producer – in the hopes that they'll do the same for you; the other is to stay as self-preservingly shtum as they will when it comes to your turn.

Understanding what they want

It's easier to see the Producer's point at some times than at others. Even the most precious writer can get their head around having inadvertently written a line that could be misconstrued or that sounds leaden when it's read aloud. Most can tolerate the substitution of a specific word for one of the same meaning, simply on the basis that the Producer favours it for reasons best known to him or herself.

The Producer thinks a scene should be longer – no problem. Apart from it meaning that another scene will have to be shorter. But, hey, what are they paying you for if it's not, in part, the ability to adapt? He or she thinks Desmond is a spare part in a scene and wants you to give him something to do or take him out – fine. Dolores casually wishes a neighbour good morning when she's refused to speak to him since 1962 – fair dos. The Producer's horrible uncle always used that expression and it's set his carefully capped choppers on-edge ever since – who can't relate to that? And anyway, there's always another way to skin a cat. We can't see Dolores crossing the street because by the time they record she'll be nine months pregnant in real life when the character isn't, and can therefore only be shot standing behind counters, bars, neck-high hedges, etc. – Aw, God-luv-her.

It's irksome to have to go away and tinker with any of it, but at least there's something definite to go on. However, it's the, 'I dunno, I just think the speech/scene needs a different sort of, kind of . . . you know what I mean,' deconstructive criticism that makes writers blench.

What you can be absolutely certain of is that the Producer or Script Editor has taken agin it. They can sometimes come as close to telling you why as talking about 'tone', but they can hardly ever define the different 'tone' they'd like you to go away and produce. 'It just needs to be more . . . and a bit less . . . you know what I mean?' Nope. Prodding your Producer or Script Editor into being more specific will invariably prove pointless. The piper who's calling the tune may not know why he or she doesn't like the pitch, but they don't – and so the challenge for you is to go home and find a way of doing the same thing differently. And different doesn't need to mean worse (*see* also pp. 119–20).

As difficult to counter are the objections based on the Producer's individual sensibilities, sense of humour – or lack of – and sometimes, not to put too fine a point on it, their pig-ignorance. It rankles to have to butcher a speech or a scene for what you see as no better reason than your boss's limitations. Replacing it with something feebler, less amusing and more simplistic can be a soul-destroying process. Try hard enough and you just might manage a way of re-doing it that overcomes the Producer's reservations and leaves you with a shred of self-esteem.

Sometimes, though, you simply have to accept doing a lesser job than you're capable of as part of the consequences of writing Soap, and trust that what you've lost on the swings of one episode, you'll gain on the roundabout of the next.

It helps to remember that the audience isn't going to miss your favourite line – just as they won't know that there was an alternative way of doing a particular scene. It's pointless for the Soap writer to nurse grievances about how their true talent and insight wasn't allowed to shine through; the crucial thing about any scene is that it ends up working well for the audience.

No time to stand and stare

I've never yet met a writer who actively relishes the prospect of doing their rewrites (barring those with season tickets to their local S&M club), and in recognition of this there is often almost as much time allowed for doing them as was allotted for the production of the first draft. Even so, there isn't much space for the often-recommended method of tackling rewrites, which is to stand back from the work for a while so that you can come back to it with something more akin to a fresh eye. As with the tight allotment given for completion of the first draft, the short time designated for doing Soap rewrites doesn't allow for much of a gap between finishing the work and having to deliver it. Here again, though, it pays to build in whatever set-aside time you can manage. Where the remit is really tight, you may be down to a day or even hours, but whatever scant stepping-back time you can give yourself will be of benefit. If, say, the official time for you finishing the rewritten script is last thing on Friday, make your own mental deadline for Wednesday. Use Thursday to print up a copy of the rewritten script and to check it for spelling and typing errors – no matter how many times you have checked and spell-checked the thing on screen, mistakes always magically appear when the text is on paper. Since this exercise (which is necessary in itself) is designed to distance you from the actual content, do not be tempted at this stage to alter any of the writing – concentrate only on finding and rectifying the technical errors. Go through the notes of the changes you were asked to make and check that you have addressed them all. Relax – or find some distraction – in whatever time you have left of Thursday. On the Friday, sit down with your hard copy of the script and read it from beginning to end, making a brief note of anything in the dialogue or directions that you can now see would benefit from further alteration or cutting. With the script on paper and read at a run, it will inevitably be easier to judge where the pace of the rewritten script slackens to the point of being boring or where some crucial section has been rushed.

Does it work for its living?

Where dialogue is concerned, it will become clearer even after the briefest of breathing spaces where any adjustments are needed. That line in the first draft that you thought was funny, well, amusing, well, amusing-ish and on second reading patently has no real point can go. That exchange which did no more than allow the characters to pass the time of day needs injecting with some information, sub-text or something to make it work for its living, otherwise it must go.

If they can see it, don't tell them about it

If you are writing for a television Soap, check that you have not used unnecessary wodges of dialogue to describe something that will be perfectly clear to the viewer as they watch the scene. What someone is watching or doing should be described in the stage directions. The audience doesn't need a commentary to go with it:

FROM DOLORES' POV WE SEE DESMOND CLIMBING UP ONTO THE ROOF.

DOLORES: I don't believe it. Look at Desmond, he's climbing up onto the roof. He'll kill himself.

All but 'He'll kill himself' is unnecessary and can be cut.

Dead but not necessarily buried

There is one tried-and-true tactic for rewriting that is as applicable to Soap scripts as it is to any other piece of writing: be brutal and murder your darlings. Tinkering with a scene purely in order to hang onto a line of dialogue that serves no other purpose than to please or amuse you will only prolong the agony. Invariably, what will be skewing your attempts to come at the scene from the different angle the Producer has demanded will be your determination to hang on to that pet speech. Take a deep breath and cut it and it may well be clearer where the real focus of the scene should be. Take heart from the fact that if the line was *that* good it won't suffer from being stored away for another day. Months, or even years on, seemingly forgotten little gems have a habit of gleaming at writers from the depths of their mental filing system. Retrieved, these bravely discarded darlings can and often do drop neatly into a setting that is, in fact, much more appropriate to them.

If, though, this stripping-out of darlings doesn't offer a new perspective on the scene, it's time to throw out the whole thing. Go back to the storyline and, without referring to the scene you originally wrote, write it again.

The writer–director meeting

Satisfying your Producer and/or Script Editor may not be the end of the rewriting process. On some shows the writer is offered the opportunity of another meeting: another bun fight at which to get bloated on strictly teetotal beverages, but this time between the writer and the Director. Referee and linesman are often provided in the guises of Producer and Script Editor.

Directors come in all shapes, sizes, colours and sexes. They also tend to come and go quite a lot. Soap is often seen by directors as a first rung, an interim step-up or a respectable step to rest on while they wait for their big-screen break. Writers are rarely, if ever, allowed to specify who they get to direct their episodes.

Faced with a novice so new that the price-tag's still on his stopwatch, a writer can reel in the space of a handshake between visions of a fresh new lightness-of-touch and a complete cack-handed disaster. Not that these reeling feelings are completely diluted when it comes to handing a script over to a more experienced member of the directorial team.

Since these meetings are usually held closer to the actual filming of a script, the writer might well have written several more episodes since finishing the one they've come to discuss with the Director. It's also entirely possible that they have had to yank themselves away from the preoccupation of an episode currently on the stocks. Distance and the distraction of a current episode may have lulled the writer into believing they don't much mind about how a piece of work they finished yonks ago ends up looking on screen. Such insouciance seldom sticks. Having reacquainted themselves with their long-lost offspring, all the writer's protective instincts can come rushing to the fore when confronted with this second and oh-so-crucial round of script surgery.

Confidence wobbles when the person entrusted with the job of exposing your work to millions has patently missed the point of a piece of dialogue or misinterprets an entire scene. It can collapse altogether when he or she pronounces your perfectly timed script too long and suggests cutting *the* most crucial four minutes.

But does the Director have a point?

As anxious as you are about what effect this second round of analysis (round one being the first-draft meeting) may have on your script, it pays to be open-minded. Remember that the Director is the first completely non-partisan eye to be cast over the episode. You, the writing team, the Producer and the Script

Editor will all, to some greater or lesser degree, have been involved in the conception, birth and development of the story-line. Together, out of familiarity with it, you may have come to assume a degree of knowledge or understanding of a particular storyline or character motivation that the audience simply won't possess. In other words, if the Director didn't get it, it's fair to assume that at least some of the audience won't either, so it's worth discussing whether a small rewrite might clarify matters.

Another criticism that is worth keeping your ears pricked for is the implication (or open accusation) that a scene is boring. Again, the collaboration of writing team, storyliners, *et al* may have developed a preoccupation or fascination with some topic or story-strand which may not engage the uninitiated. It's another case where some rewriting might be justified on the basis that spicing up the Director's interest will help him or her motivate the actors, who will then stand a better chance of capturing and keeping the audience's attention.

Audience attention span

While in no way espousing the view that audiences have the attention span of the average gnat, the television writer does have to take account of the fact that only a small percentage of any audience will be sitting glued to every word that's transmitted. Soap scenes will often be competing with all manner of domestic distractions and interruptions and need to maintain both pace and interest to stand a chance of surviving. Where a director is suggesting that – despite their best efforts – a scene is in danger of flagging to a fatal degree, it merits another serious look.

Whose script is it anyway?

Whatever compromises, improvements and changes come out of the writer–director meeting, they are usually the last the writer has by way of input. The majority of Soap directors do not relish having the writer around during rehearsals and/or recordings and so, although you may be tolerated if you insist on turning up, you will invariably feel that you're in the way. This isn't just to do with how little time Soap schedules afford for directors and crew to be dealing with another somebody on set; it is a question of professional etiquette. Your job was to write; theirs is to bring their own area of expertise to bear in making what you wrote come to life.

Of course, this feeling of ultimate powerlessness over the presentation of the finished product is common to writers of all ilks. Apart from the novel (and even that can be influenced by the editing process), few inventions get to fly straight from the writer's head onto the stage, air-waves or screen. Certainly in television, where so many subsequent disciplines need to be applied – lighting, camera, sound, direction, performance – it isn't realistic for a writer to get too autocratically attached to their script. Achieving a healthy degree of indifference is, however, easier said than done, especially since producers expect the writer to care passionately about what they write, only to accuse them of caring to a precious degree when it comes to trying to preserve the integrity of what they've written.

It's sometimes difficult to hang on to a definition of the writer's role when its importance fluctuates so confusingly between the sentiment that, 'If it ain't on the page, it ain't on the stage,' and being seen as 'the necessary weevil'. I suppose what keeps most Soap writers from headbutting their screens on a fatally brain-damaging scale are those moments when, despite everything, a scene works the way they intended. And, it has to be acknowledged, when a less than brilliant scene is made to work far better than it deserved due to acute editing, skilful direction and masterly performances.

Number of drafts

On some shows it is expected that this second draft will be the definitive one, since there isn't time for a third. On other shows, such as the aforementioned *Eastenders*, they may allow for up to six drafts but, whatever the brief, the writer must observe it. Writers whose scripts need surgery beyond the allowed number of drafts tend not to last terribly long. At whatever point a workable draft is accepted, that's when all those most arduous and least enjoyable bits of the process are put aside. They need to be, since it'll be just about coming round to the next storyline meeting and the next lot of commissions.

9. Health Warnings

As well as many benefits, there are risks attached to being a writer of Soap, especially on a long-term basis. To analyse them, we need to flashback to the Introduction and people's motives for wanting to be a Soap writer:

- They admire a particular show and want to be involved in it.
- They like the show well enough, and the prospect of big audiences and regular bucks every bit as much.
- They see it as honest bread-and-butter toil that will buy them time to write what they *really* want to write.
- They despise everything about it – except the money.

On the face of it, there should be least risk of damage to those who have a real regard for the programme they write for. However, the potential danger here is that they will care too much about something over which they have too little control. No single person on a Soap will get their own way over everything all of the time. (And believe me, I tried.) Even a producer's finest and best intentions will not always be achievable due to the collaborative nature of the process, the restrictions of budget and the content limitations imposed by those who buy the programme.

At the other end of the scale, the deeply cynical are the most immune from feeling that their personal artistic integrity is being harmed. However, the danger of their being in too great a majority on any show is that their underlying disregard for the audience and for what they give them will eventually show through. The show starts to ring hollow in the ears of even the most ardent of fans and they begin to look elsewhere for a show that doesn't insult their intelligence to an unbearable degree.

So, caring too much or too little can prove hazardous to the individual writer and/or the show as a whole. It should stand to reason, then, that somewhere between these extremes there is a sane, safe place for writers of Soap to be. Doing as honourable a job as possible within Soap's limitations, relishing their contribution to a collaborative effort, and using the rewards to finance the self-generated stuff should be as beneficial to the writer as to the show. And I would like to be able to tell you that this happy balance is easy to achieve, but it isn't.

As you will have gathered, the schedule for regular Soap writers is a pretty punishing one. Working flat out to some of the tightest of television deadlines can, in itself, be exhausting. Add to this the seemingly endless round of meetings a writer may be expected to attend, the reworking for rewrites and sometimes several drafts, and there can be little or no time and energy left for creating that play or *the* novel.

Becoming one of that tiny proportion of writers who manage to live by their writing earnings alone makes offers of lucrative Soap commissions hard to turn down. And the more a writer goes on accepting commissions, the harder it gets to decline the chance of staying in regular employment. Being mere mortals, many previously under-rewarded writers fall quickly into the trap of winding up their standard of living to match their new earnings. Before they know where they are, quitting Soap means being unable to maintain the comfortable lifestyle they have so rapidly become accustomed to.

It's nice to be needed

But decisions about writing for Soap aren't just about money. In addition to the financial lifeline that contributing regularly to Soap gives a writer, there is the rarity of feeling needed. Since so much writing outside Soap is self-motivated and 'on spec', the prospect of a return to the cold world where no-one is clamouring for your output can be a daunting one.

Losing the edge

A very astute radio drama producer used to stop me, along with all of his other writers, in our tracks if any of us tried to outline something we were planning to write. 'Don't tell me about it – write it.' He knew, you see, that in telling him about a play we risked getting it out of our system to the point where there was no longer any need to write it. When it comes to Soap there can be something of a similar risk element: a tendency for writers used to regular Soap involvement to feel that they have, at one time or another, written every angle of every story there is. They may well have been party to writing about a particular issue in less breadth and depth than they would have liked, but the fact is that they have taken a glancing blow at the topic and, in effect, taken the edge off their creative drive to tackle it from an individual perspective.

Solitary confinement

Yet another potential pitfall for those Soap writers involved in any amount of storyline meetings lies in how unconsciously accustomed they can become to having to defend their ideas to the group. Back in solitary confinement with only their own imaginations to argue against, writers too used to committee planning can have problems with taking sole responsibility for deciding which avenue of development an idea should take.

What a coincidence

Writing too much and too long for Soaps can also lead to the writer losing sight of that valuable device – coincidence. In the Soap genre, the overuse of coincidence undermines the intention to reflect real life. And the more real a Soap attempts to be, the more careful it is about using the tool of happenstance simply to facilitate plot progression. In the novel or on stage we often take completely for granted some quite extraordinary coincidences, whereas in Soap a writer might have been laughed out of court for daring to suggest them. Here again, back at the desk with only a blank screen and a solo flight of creativity to contemplate, the writer too accustomed to Soap may find it hard to convince themselves that coincidence is a viable option.

But the good news is. . .

None of this is to say that a satisfactory balance can't be achieved or that Soap is all bad news for the writer. Soap has discovered and supported some of the most exciting contemporary writing talents up to the point where they were ready to fly off to individual success, and has kept many a competent scriptwriter with no aspirations outside the genre in regular, worthwhile work.

Soap does teach the writer to be disciplined both in speech and storytelling terms – a valuable asset to any and every other form of writing. And on a different sort of discipline front, Soap teaches stamina and encourages routine in those who, otherwise, might mistakenly believe that the job of a writer entails drifting around waiting for will-power as well as inspiration to strike. Since the old adage that writing is ten per cent inspiration and 90 per cent perspiration is true, whatever the writer sets out to do in tandem with – or instead of – Soap will never be achieved without this work ethic.

And last but not least of Soap's virtues is the sheer enormity of its audience. On those occasions when a writer gets to say something the way they want to say it, few get the chance to offer up this act of communication to so many.

So, if none of this has deterred you and you would like to try your hand at an episode of Soap, the following sections contain a dummy storyline breakdown and a script to illustrate one way in which the breakdown could be interpreted.

10. Sample Storyline Breakdown

As covered in Chapter 2, a writer who has been offered a commission for an episode of Soap will almost certainly be supplied with some sort of storyline breakdown or story document to work from. Storyline breakdowns vary from Soap to Soap in how extensively they describe and dictate the action of a given episode. Some are very specific and dictate both the order of scenes and what action takes place within them.

However, I have based the construction of an episode of the invented show *Lansdown* on the other sort of storyline breakdown. What follows, then, is the type of format that calls for the writer to create their own structure as well as the dialogue. The first page of a storyline breakdown sometimes specifies which characters, sets and locations are to be used and I have worked on this principle for the invented Soap. If you attempt to write your own practice version of the episode (*see* Chapter 11, *Sample Script*), remember that you must not exceed or alter the given allocation of sets, locations and characters. By the same token, you must cover all the storyline points and use all the characters you have been allotted.

Bearing in mind that a real Soap would almost certainly have a longer character list, and several more ongoing minor and major background stories that need to be kept on the boil, the following mock storyline breakdown should serve to demonstrate the crucial elements of constructing a script to a given Soap template.

(SAMPLE) STORYLINE: 'LANSDOWN' EPISODE 2324

T/X[1] MONDAY, 4TH JULY, 2001 Sunrise: 06.00 hrs/Sunset: 21.50 hrs[2]

MAJOR CHARACTERS:	Desmond Dent
	Dolores Dent
	Philippa Dent
	Greg Burton
	Sonia Stafford
	Gavin Stafford
	Susan Hargrove
	Nicola Hargrove
MINOR CHARACTERS:[3]	Rev. Cox
	Debra Thorn
	Brad Stafford
	Simon Kinna
	Salon Client 1
	Salon Client 2
INT. SETS:	Dent Kitchen
	Cutz Salon
	Stafford Sitting Room
	Stafford Kitchen
	Hargrove Bathroom
	Hargrove Back Bedroom
EXT. SETS:	Dents' Rear Patio
	Street o/s Hargrove Front Door
LOCATIONS:	Baptist Chapel
EVENTS:	Desmond Dent's Birthday
	American Independence Day

[1]T/X is shorthand for the date the episode will be transmitted. A helpful reminder, since the episode may be being written as much as six months in advance.

[2]To remind the writer when setting scene times whether they will be asking for day or night shoots.

[3]Not necessarily minor in importance, but of relatively minor significance in this particular episode.

'LANSDOWN' STORYLINE – EPISODE 2324

THE DENTS

Desmond has ended his affair with Susan Hargrove (EP. 2323). He feels free to enjoy his birthday in the bosom of his family.

Both his wife and daughter seem distracted and take little account of it being his special day.

Dolores still suspects something is bothering Phillipa. Phillipa goes to Nicola Hargrove for advice but unwittingly gets Nicola into further trouble with her boss.

Dolores arrives at the chapel to arrange the flowers. Rev. Cox mentions, in all innocence, having seen Desmond with a young woman (EP. 2320). Dolores deduces it was Susan Hargrove and her suspicions are aroused.

Back at home, Dolores confronts Desmond about why he was with Susan. He lies unconvincingly, she goes off to try to get the truth from Susan. He runs after her to try to stop her.

In the aftermath of Desmond's confession on the Hargrove doorstep and an unconscious Susan being taken off to hospital, the Dents return home rowing bitterly.

They are met by Phillipa – and her boyfriend Simon, who announces that they are moving in together and that Simon is married. Will Dolores reveal Desmond's infidelity to their daughter? (<u>END OF EPISODE HOOK</u>)

SUSAN AND NICOLA HARGROVE

Susan is deeply depressed. She finds some old sleeping pills and goes back to bed, taking the bottle of pills with her.

Nicola is at work in the salon. She is oblivious to her sister's state of mind. Her own battle with Debra about the menial nature of the work she is being given is ongoing.

Debra is annoyed when Greg Burton turns up at the salon to ask Nicola if she knows her sister's whereabouts. Nicola has no idea where Susan is or why she didn't go to work and doesn't seem concerned.

Phillipa Dent arrives at the salon to talk to Nicola. It sparks more friction between Nicola and Debra and Nicola quits her job.

THE STAFFORDS

Gavin is still furious about Brad's school refusing to take him on any future school trips. His decision to keep Brad off school (PREVIOUS HOOK EP. 2323) until they reverse their decision still stands.

Sonia has sympathy with the school's decision. She is still waiting to hear if she has got the new job she has applied for.

Sonia hears that she has got the job – but how can she take it if Brad is going to be kept away from school indefinitely? (END OF PART ONE HOOK)

Brad, despite his last school holiday experience of falling into a coma, is still rebelling about taking responsibility for his diabetic regime.

Gavin finds a babysitter for Brad, but Sonia isn't sure it's the solution.

GREG BURTON

Greg can't fathom why Susan has not turned in for work. Anxious following the previous night's telephone conversation he had with Susan (EP. 2323), during which she sounded depressed, he calls at her home. Getting no response, Greg sets off to the salon to see if Nicola knows where her sister is.

Nicola doesn't know where Susan is and dismisses his concern when Greg hints at the previous evening's depressed phone call.

Greg goes back to the Hargrove house. Again he gets no reply. He is about to leave when an angry Dolores arrives, having come to try to get the truth from Susan about why she was seen with Desmond. Desmond, who has hurried out to stop Dolores, panics and reveals that he had been seeing Susan but that he broke it off yesterday.

Greg, having heard this, is convinced that Susan is inside the house and may have tried to kill herself. Greg smashes a glass pane in the front door. Upstairs he finds Susan unconscious. Nicola arrives home in time to accompany Susan in the ambulance.

An anxious Greg is left watching them go.

11. Sample Script

Before you read on

What follows is a sample script based on the storyline breakdown in Chapter 10. You may wish to practise your hand at writing the episode before going on to read the version I have written.

If you feel confident enough, tackle the writing of the episode from start to finish. If you feel you need to read yourself into the general flow of the episode before you have a go, read up until the end of part one and no further and then attempt your own version of part two. When you have completed the writing of your own version of the whole or half episode it might be useful to read my mock script for comparative purposes. By this, I don't mean that you need or should compare styles of writing. The fact that your style may differ from mine doesn't mean it is any better or worse as, in terms of the aptness and acceptability of writing styles, this could differ hugely from Soap to Soap. For the purpose of this suggested exercise, the benefit of checking my version in relation to yours is more a matter of essential mechanics. What you will be looking to confirm is that you have covered all the plot points in the storyline breakdown using only the characters, sets and locations given on the front page, and that you have successfully managed to manoeuvre the episode towards the given hook or hooks.

For *Lansdown*, our invented show, I have assumed a budget that would allow the writer between 20 and 25 scenes.

Timing a script

It's patently not a good idea to submit a script (even – probably especially – as a sample submission) that is either ludicrously overlong or underruns by several minutes. If, as was suggested earlier, you are submitting a piece of the same duration as the show you have ambitions to write for, you need to demonstrate that you have the necessary sense of timing. In the real world of Soap-writing, the writer who submits too long a script invites the heartbreak of seeing some good stuff get the chop. Where a Soap professional's script is too short it may mean that the whole script structure will come into question and a major rewrite will be on the cards.

Unfortunately, estimating the timing of a script is by no means an exact science. One way of calculating script length is to read it out loud very slowly, pacing out (physically if possible, mentally if not) all the action it contains. And very slowly means just that because, by some mysterious process, a script invariably ends up lengthening in production.

Because of the limitations of space in this book it has not been practical to lay out an entire script in exactly the way it would normally be formatted. But, as a general rule of thumb, the following sample script – **with each new scene starting on a new page, using wider margins, double-line spacing and double-line spacing times two between speeches** – would run to between 58 and 60 pages – which should make for around 23 minutes on screen. This is around the required length for a half-hour Soap given that titles, credits and the commercial break will bring the piece up to 30 minutes (*see* also page 48).

Obviously, timing scripts for a particular show gets easier with practice, but even seasoned Soap writers are often surprised when a director declares that the read-through (the first stage of rehearsals when actors simply sit and read the script aloud) took several minutes longer than the writer thought it would.

Remember too that each show has its own in-house preference when it comes to script layout and that the following composite version is somewhat condensed. If you are intending to submit a mock episode, try to lay hands on an old script and follow its particular format. If you can't get hold of one of the show's scripts, the following composite template should serve you well enough.

Sample script

-1-

<u>Sc. 01   (EXT.)   STREET O/S HARGROVES'   09.30</u>

<u>GREG</u> SLAMS HIS CAR DOOR. HE HURRIES ANXIOUSLY
TOWARDS THE HARGROVE FRONT DOOR AND RINGS
THE BELL. GETTING NO REPLY, HE LOOKS UP AT THE
BEDROOM WINDOW. THE CURTAINS ARE CLOSED.
<u>GREG</u> RINGS THE BELL AGAIN.

<u>GAVIN</u>, PASSING ON HIS WAY HOME WITH NEWLY
BOUGHT NEWSPAPER, CALLS LIGHTHEARTEDLY TO
<u>GREG</u>.

1.   GAVIN: Like trying to wake the dead, eh?

2.   GREG: (HIDING HIS ANXIETY) Yeah.

3.   GAVIN: These young ones. Don't know they're born.

<u>GREG</u> NODS BUT DOESN'T WANT TO CHAT. HE RINGS
THE BELL AGAIN.

4.   GAVIN: I'd done a paper-round by the time our Brad crawls
out of his pit. Be even worse now. Us having to keep him off
school.

5.   GREG: (FOR THE SAKE OF POLITENESS) Lot of it about –
this bug-thing.

-2-

1.   GAVIN: (MOMENTARILY CONFUSED) Oh, no. Brad's not
ill. Well, there's his diabetes. But that's a condition, not an
illness. Not that his teachers can see it. Can you believe them?
Refusing to take the kid on a school trip?

2.   GREG: (STARTING BACK TO HIS CAR) Shame. Sorry, need
to see if Nicola knows where Susan's got to. Didn't turn in for
work.

3.   GAVIN: Maybe she's down with the bug.

132

4.   GREG: (GETTING INTO CAR) Could be. See you, Gavin.

5.   GAVIN: (WAVING NEWSPAPER IN FAREWELL) Cheers.
      And I hope Susan's all right when you find her.

ON GREG, SERIOUSLY CONCERNED ABOUT THE SAME
THING BUT FOR DIFFERENT REASONS.

CUT TO:

-3-

<u>Sc. 02   (INT.)   HARGROVE BACK BEDROOM   09.35</u>

<u>SUSAN</u>, WEARING NIGHTDRESS AND DISHEVELLED
FROM A SLEEPLESS NIGHT, DRAWS BACK HER BED-
ROOM CURTAIN A LITTLE. FROM HER POV WE SEE
<u>DESMOND</u> OUTSIDE ON THE NEXT DOOR PATIO.
<u>SUSAN</u> WATCHES AS <u>DOLORES</u> COMES OUTSIDE AND
HANDS <u>DESMOND</u> A CUP OF COFFEE. A SMILING
<u>DESMOND</u> PECKS <u>DOLORES</u> ON THE CHEEK.
MISERABLE WITH HURT AND JEALOUSY, <u>SUSAN</u> SHUTS
THE CURTAIN.

ON <u>SUSAN</u>'S UNHAPPINESS.

CUT TO:

-4-

<u>Sc. 03   (INT.)   STAFFORD KITCHEN   09.40</u>

<u>SONIA</u> SHOUTS LOUDLY AT THE CEILING.

1.   SONIA: Brad!! I'll not tell you again!

<u>GAVIN</u> ENTERS CARRYING NEWSPAPER AND MAIL.
<u>SONIA</u> WILL CLEAR BREAKFAST DISHES/LOAD
DISHWASHER.

2.   GAVIN: He'd sleep through the Apocolypse, that boy.

3.   SONIA: (DEFEATED) Tell me about it. (AS <u>GAVIN</u> SIFTS
      THROUGH POST) Anything for me?

4.   GAVIN: Nope.

133

5. SONIA: (ANXIOUS) What am I going to do, Gav? If they do offer me the job?

6. GAVIN: (CONFUSED) Celebrate? You haven't changed your mind about wanting to do it?

7. SONIA: 'Course not. But they were looking for an immediate starter.

8. GAVIN: So?

-5-

1. SONIA: So, how am I supposed to do that with Brad off school?

2. GAVIN: (SHRUGS) We'd have to work that one out for when he was on holiday –

3. SONIA: (IRRITATED) But this isn't holidays, is it? This is a kid who's missing school indefinitely. Thanks to you.

4. GAVIN: And thank you for the wifely support.

5. SONIA: You're the one who made the big dramatic gesture – but I'm the one who has to suffer the consequences.

6. GAVIN: (TRYING TO PLACATE) Trust me. If you're offered the job, I'm not going to let this nonsense with Brad's school stop you getting back to work.

7. SONIA: Oh, so you'll give up your job then? Because there's no way Brad's being left on his own all day.

8. GAVIN: Sonia, the boy's nearly thirteen.

9. SONIA: Just like he was when he ignored his diet and put himself into a diabetic coma. No wonder the school don't want the responsibility of him on another holiday. He could have died.

-6-

1. GAVIN: But he didn't, did he? And one mistake doesn't give his headmaster the right to deny the boy another trip with his mates.

2.   SONIA: (SULLEN) He probably wouldn't even have wanted to go on the next trip to – where is it? – (WITH DISDAIN) – Denmark?

3.   GAVIN: That's not the point.

4.   SONIA: (SARCASTIC) Too right. The point is (AS SHE EXITS) you're even more pig-headed than your son.

GAVIN IS LEFT TO STEW. HE WINCES AS HE HEARS SONIA CALLING UPSTAIRS AGAIN.

5.   SONIA: (OOV) Brad!! If I have to come up there, you'll be sorry!

ON A DISPIRITED GAVIN.

                                                    CUT TO:

-7-

Sc. 04   (INT.)   CUTZ SALON   10.00

NICOLA IS CLEANING BACK-WASH BASINS. DEBRA IS ACROSS THE SALON POSITIONING A SPIDER-HEAT LAMP OVER THE PLASTIC-BAGGED HEAD OF CLIENT. DEBRA EYES NICOLA TO MAKE SURE SHE'S BEING SUITABLY INDUSTRIOUS. ON THE COUNTER THERE IS AN AMATEUR DISPLAY OF AMERICAN FLAGS, RED, WHITE & BLUE BALLOONS, ETC. TO MARK INDEPENDENCE DAY.

1.   DEBRA: (TO CLIENT) All right for you, Mrs T? Got your mags there? (THE CLIENT NODS) Excellento. (MOVING OFF) Be about twenty minutes. I've put your pinger on.

DEBRA COMES TO INSPECT THE BACK-WASH BASINS. HER PRESENCE SETS NICOLA'S TEETH ON EDGE.

2.   DEBRA: See if Mrs T would like a coffee, please, Nicola.

3.   NICOLA: Already did – and she didn't.

4.   DEBRA: Then perhaps you'd see if she's changed her mind.

135

NICOLA RAISES HER EYES HEAVENWARDS AND STARTS
TOWARDS CLIENT.

-8-

1. DEBRA: (TO STOP NICOLA AND INDICATING
    CLEANING FLUID/CLOTH LEFT ON BACK-WASH) When
    you've put this away, if you don't mind, Nicola.

    NICOLA, WITH MINIMAL GRACE, RETURNS TO SWEEP
    CLEANING STUFF OFF BASIN THEN EXITS TO STAFF
    ROOM. GREG ENTERS. DEBRA GOES TO DEAL WITH
    HIM. (DEBRA DOES NOT KNOW HIM.)

2. GREG: Morning. I just wondered if –

3. DEBRA: Oh, I'm awfully sorry, but I'm not unisex.

4. GREG: Er, no, I wasn't wanting . . . (A HAIRCUT) I just
    wondered if –

5. DEBRA: (GRANDLY) And I have my regular suppliers for
    products.

6. GREG: No, I'm not . . . (SELLING ANYTHING)

    NICOLA ENTERS FROM STAFF-ROOM. GREG LOOKS
    RELIEVED.

7. NICOLA: (SURPRISED) Greg. Hi.

8. DEBRA: (MOCK POLITE TO GREG) Staff aren't encouraged
    to socialise in working hours. Especially when we're so busy.

-9-

GREG POINTEDLY TAKES IN SALON WHICH IS EMPTY
BUT FOR ONE CLIENT.

1   GREG: This won't take more than a sec. (TO NICOLA) Sorry
    about this. I just wondered if Susan was okay.

2. NICOLA: (MILD SURPRISE) Isn't she at work?

    DEBRA TUTS AND HEADS OFF TO READJUST HEAT-
    LAMPS OVER HER CLIENT.

3.   DEBRA: I'm sure I don't need to remind you that we've got two highlights and a demi-wave due, Nicola.

4.   NICOLA: No, Mrs Thorn. (TO <u>GREG</u>) Have you been to the house?

5.   GREG: Couldn't get any answer. Wondered if she might be – I don't know – ill or something. The front bedroom curtains are still shut.

6.   NICOLA: (AMUSED) Oh, that's me – slut. Suzie's room's at the back.

7.   GREG: You'd think she'd still hear the door bell, though.

-10-

1.   NICOLA: Probably just overslept. I know it's not like her but (JOKES) hey, maybe she's human after all.

2.   GREG: (WORRIED BUT TRYING NOT TO ALARM <u>NICOLA</u>) Yeah. I'll go try again. (TURNS TO GO THEN HESITATES) She seemed okay to you, though? Last night, I mean?

<u>DEBRA</u>, IN THE BACKGROUND, IS PREPARING A BLEACH TROLLEY AND LOOKING INCREASINGLY IRRITATED.

3.   NICOLA: She'd gone to bed by the time I got in. (CURIOUS) Why? Is there some reason she shouldn't be okay?

4.   GREG: (FIBBING TO REASSURE) No. Just when I rang last night, she sounded . . . bit down, that's all.

<u>NICOLA</u>'S CURIOSITY INCREASES BUT <u>DEBRA</u>'S DISAPPROVING CALL STOPS HER PURSUING THE MATTER.

5.   DEBRA: If it's not cramping your style, Nicola – I will be needing tin-foils ready for Mrs Bell.

6.   NICOLA: (IRRITABLY) I'm just coming, okay?

GREG DOESN'T WANT TO GET NICOLA INTO FURTHER BOTHER WITH HER BOSS AND SO STARTS OUT OF THE SALON.

1. GREG: (TO DEBRA) My fault. Sorry. (THEN TO NICOLA) Don't worry. You're probably right about her oversleeping. I'll go and give her another try.

2. NICOLA: (AS GREG EXITS) Okay. See you.

A LOOK OF MILD CONCERN STARTS TO DAWN ON NICOLA'S FACE BUT DEBRA CALLS OVER TO HER AGAIN.

3. DEBRA: Weren't you going to ask Mrs T about that coffee, Nicola?

NICOLA, DISTRACTED FROM CURIOSITY ABOUT HER SISTER, TRUDGES TOWARDS THE CLIENT.

4. NICOLA: Yes, Mrs Thorn. Just doing it, Mrs Thorn.

ON DEBRA'S TIGHT-LIPPED SMILE AT NICOLA'S BARELY CONCEALED INSOLENCE.

CUT TO:

-12-

Sc. 05   (INT.)   DENT KITCHEN   10.15

DESMOND HAS JUST UNWRAPPED A BEIGE SWEATER – A GIFT THAT IS ALMOST IDENTICAL TO THE SWEATER HE IS WEARING. DOLORES LOOKS ON, EMBARRASSED BY HER LACK OF ORIGINALITY. THERE ARE FOUR OPENED BIRTHDAY CARDS ON THE TABLE.

1. DOLORES: I don't mind if you want to change it. Honestly.

2. DESMOND: (COVERING DISAPPOINTMENT) No, it's ... just what I needed. (HE GIVES HER A GENUINELY AFFECTIONATE PECK ON THE CHEEK) Thanks, Doll. So – where do you fancy for my birthday lunch then, eh?

3. DOLORES: (EMBARRASSED/APOLOGETIC) Desmond, I can't.

DESMOND LOOKS CRESTFALLEN.

4. DOLORES: The chapel's got a wedding on and I said I'd do the flowers.

5. DESMOND: But we always do a birthday lunch out. I've given myself the day off for it.

-13-

1. DOLORES: I know and I'm sorry. It's just that Connie's away and Reverend Cox rang to see if I could fill in. And I'd said yes (LAMELY) before I remembered –

2. DESMOND: (HURT) That it was my birthday. It's not like it's an easy one to forget, is it? The fourth of July.

3. DOLORES: I've said I'm sorry. There just seems to have been so much going on. What with you setting up working from home and Philippa's shifts changing every five minutes.

4. DESMOND: At least this agency nursing's better paid.

5. DOLORES: Mmm. But she does seem on edge somehow. As if there's something bothering her. Not that I can get her to talk about it.

PHILIPPA ENTERS. SHE IS WEARING NURSING UNIFORM. SHE IS OBVIOUSLY RUNNING LATE AS SHE SEARCHES FOR HER CAR KEYS.

DESMOND BEAMS IN ANTICIPATION OF BIRTHDAY GREETINGS.

6. DESMOND: Good morning!

-14-

1. PHILIPPA: (ROOTING IN HANDBAG FOR CAR KEYS) Try saying that on six hours sleep. (FINDS KEYS) Right, I'm off.

    DESMOND LOOKS DISAPPOINTED. PHILIPPA PLONKS A KISS ON HIS HEAD IN PASSING AND NOTICES BIRTHDAY CARDS.

2. PHILIPPA: (PRETENDING TO HAVE REMEMBERED) Hey, yeah and happy birthday! I thought I'd give you your pressy when I get back, if that's okay. I'm only covering for a couple of hours.

3. DESMOND: (DISGUISING DISAPPOINTMENT) Sure. Fine.

4. PHILIPPA: So I've got time to see you open it and everything. I hadn't forgotten – honestly.

5. DESMOND: (PRETENDING TO BELIEVE HER) No, 'course you hadn't. Don't go making yourself late. I'll see you later.

6. PHILIPPA: (EXITING) See you later then, Birthday Boy. Bye, Mum.

7. DOLORES: (PUTTING ON HER COAT AND TO PHILIPPA) Bye, love.

8. DESMOND: She seems all right to me. Apart from the congenital memory loss.

-15-

1. DOLORES: (IGNORING THE IMPLIED SLIGHT) Mmm, well, I still think there's something bothering her. (THEN NOTICING DESMOND'S DEJECTION AT NOT BEING CENTRE OF ATTENTION) Aw, I'm sorry about your birthday lunch.

2. DESMOND: Oh, well. What's another birthday when you get to my age?

    DOLORES CHECKS SHE'S GOT SCISSORS, FLORIST WIRE, ETC. IN HER SHOPPING BAG.

3.   DOLORES: We just all seem to have been so busy lately. You as much as any of us – out every night trying to build your client list up. (JOKINGLY) I was starting to think you must be having an affair or something.

4.   DESMOND: (MANAGING A WEAK SMILE) Don't be daft.

DOLORES PAUSES ON HER WAY OUT.

5.   DOLORES: If I get my skates on, I could have these flowers done by half-one. Why don't you meet me at the chapel and we'll go on somewhere?

6.   DESMOND: (PLEASANTLY BUT THE PARTY MOOD HAS PASSED) No – don't worry. We'll do it another day.

-16-

1.   DOLORES: I'll make us something nice for supper then, eh? Just you and me.

DESMOND SMILES IN AGREEMENT/FAREWELL. DOLORES EXITS. LOOKING LESS THAN ECSTATIC AT THE THOUGHT OF A QUIET NIGHT IN WITH HIS WIFE, DESMOND STANDS HIS BIRTHDAY CARD FROM DOLORES UP ON THE KITCHEN TABLE. THE SENTIMENT ON THE FRONT IS OF THE JOKEY, MILDLY INSULTING VARIETY – 'TO MY OLD MAN.'

CUT TO:

-17-

Sc. 06   (INT.)   HARGROVE BATHROOM   10.30

SUSAN OPENS THE BATHROOM CABINET. SHE REMOVES A COSMETIC BOTTLE OR TWO AND TAKES OUT AN ENVELOPE THAT SHE HAD HIDDEN AT THE BACK OF THE CABINET. SHE DRAWS A BIRTHDAY CARD FROM THE ENVELOPE. THE FRONT OF IT READS 'TO MY DEAREST DARLING'. IN A BURST OF ANGUISH, SUSAN TEARS UP THE CARD. SHE THROWS THE PIECES INTO THE LAVATORY AND TRIES TO FLUSH THEM AWAY. REALISING HOW FUTILE A GESTURE IT IS, SUSAN STARTS TO PUT BOTTLES BACK INTO THE CABINET.

141

SHE IS ABOUT TO CLOSE THE CABINET DOOR WHEN
SHE SEES A BOTTLE OF PILLS.

THE DOORBELL RINGS.

SUSAN MOMENTARILY CONSIDERS RESPONDING TO
IT, BUT THEN LOOKS BACK AT THE PILL BOTTLE AND
TAKES IT FROM THE CABINET.

ON SUSAN'S HAND, CLOSING AROUND THE BOTTLE
OF PILLS.

CUT TO:

-18-

Sc. 07   (INT.)   STAFFORD SITTING ROOM   10.40

BRAD, WEARING SLEEP T-SHIRT AND BOXERS, IS
SLUMPED ON THE SOFA. BARE FEET UP ON COFFEE
TABLE, HE YAWNS JAW-BREAKINGLY AS HE FLICKS
THROUGH A COMPUTER MAGAZINE. SONIA ENTERS
CARRYING VACUUM CLEANER. SHE SIGHS AT THE
UNKEMPT VISION OF IDLENESS THAT IS HER SON.

1.   SONIA: Haven't you even had your shower yet?

BRAD KEEPS ON READING HIS MAGAZINE.

2.   BRAD: Just going.

3.   SONIA: (PLUGGING IN VACUUM CLEANER AND
NODDING AT BRAD'S FEET) Do you want a plate for those?

BRAD SIGHS SULKILY AND TAKES HIS FEET OFF THE
TABLE.

GAVIN COMES TO SITTING ROOM DOOR AND IS
PLEASED TO SEE BRAD.

4.   GAVIN: Ah, you're up?

19

1. SONIA: If you can call it that. (TO <u>BRAD</u>) I'll bet you haven't done your jab yet either, have you?

2. BRAD: (SULLEN) I was just going to – all-right?

    <u>SONIA</u> LOOKS ANXIOUS/ANNOYED. <u>GAVIN</u> FORESEES A ROW AND TRIES TO CIRCUMVENT IT.

3. GAVIN: (BRIGHTLY TO <u>BRAD</u>) Why don't you grab a shower and come for a ride down to the wholesalers with me?

    <u>BRAD</u> LOOKS BRIEFLY ENLIVENED BUT <u>SONIA</u> SCOTCHES THE SUGGESTION.

4   SONIA: Oh, very educational. The deal was, if he was off school he'd be doing some revising.

5. BRAD: Not my fault I'm off school, is it?

    <u>SONIA</u> GIVES <u>GAVIN</u> A KNOWING LOOK. <u>GAVIN</u> LOOKS UNCOMFORTABLE. HE IS RESCUED BY THE TELEPHONE STARTING TO RING. <u>GAVIN</u> MOVES TOWARDS IT.

6. SONIA: (INTERCEPTING HIM) No, let me. It might be about the job.

20

<u>SONIA</u> REACHES THE PHONE. SHE TAKES A DEEP BREATH, HOLDS UP CROSSED FINGERS AND THEN PICKS UP THE RECEIVER.

1. SONIA: Hello? (PAUSE) Yes, it is. (LISTENS AND LOOKS PERPLEXED) Oh, er, yes. Yes, he is. Hang on. (HOLDS RECEIVER OUT TO <u>GAVIN</u>) Somebody called Simmonds – says he's a reporter on the Evening Argus.

ON <u>GAVIN</u>, SURPRISED AND CURIOUS.

                                        CUT TO:

<u>Sc. 08   (INT.)   BAPTIST CHAPEL   11.15</u>

<u>DOLORES</u> IS ARRANGING FLOWERS BY THE SIMPLE
ALTAR. SHE STANDS BACK TO EXAMINE HER EFFORTS
AND DOESN'T LOOK OVERLY IMPRESSED. <u>REVEREND
COX</u> ENTERS. HE WEARS CARDIGAN AND JEANS WITH
HIS DOG-COLLAR AND IS CARRYING AN OIL CAN.

1   REV. COX: (OF FLOWERS) Wow!

2.   DOLORES: I'm not sure. Do you think it needs something else?

3.   REV. COX: No. I like it. Less is more, as they say.

4.   DOLORES: (UNCONVINCED) Minimalism isn't to
everyone's taste, though, is it?

5.   REV. COX: (CHUCKLES) Then they shouldn't choose to get
hitched in my chapel. We Baptists <u>invented</u> chucking out the
chintz.

<u>DOLORES</u> SMILES/STARTS TO GATHER UP FLOWER-
ARRANGING KIT.

<u>REV. COX</u> STARTS TO OIL HINGES ON DOOR TO VESTRY.

6.   DOLORES: Oh, well, if you're sure it'll do, I'll get started on
the pew ends. If I'd known I was going to get finished so soon I
could have gone with Desmond for his birthday lunch.

-22-

1.   REV. COX: Oh, a birthday! Tell him many happy returns.

<u>DOLORES</u> ACKNOWLEDGES WITH A SMILE AND
STARTS ON DECORATING PEW ENDS WITH FOLIAGE.
<u>REV. COX</u> TESTS THE EFFECT OF OILED DOOR HINGES.

2.   REV. COX: How's Desmond doing with the freelancing?

3.   DOLORES: Fine. Well, it'll take a time for him to build up a
really decent client list. But working from home means he's got
no overheads to worry about.

4.   REV. COX: And I suppose he's only got himself and his
      assistant to pay. Seems a nice young woman.

DOLORES HAD BEEN PAYING SCANT ATTENTION AND
NOW THINKS SHE MAY HAVE MISHEARD.

5.   DOLORES: Who? Sorry?

6   REV. COX: Desmond's new assistant. I bumped into them in
      town. Monday evening it would be. She seems a nice, sensible
      sort of girl, doesn't she?

-23-

1.   DOLORES: (CASUALLY TO MASK DAWNING SUSPICION)
      Oh, that's right. Des said they were meeting up. But, er, I
      haven't actually met her yet. In fact, I can't even think what
      Des said her name was.

2.   REV. COX: (TRYING TO RECALL) I remember thinking she
      looked Irish – all that lovely auburn hair. But I can't, for the
      life of me, remember … (HER NAME)

3.   DOLORES: (TO HERSELF AS SHE REALISES) Susan.

4.   REV. COX: That's it! Susan.

PRIVATELY, DOLORES' HEART SINKS. SHE HASTILY
STARTS TO GATHER UP FOLIAGE AND SCISSORS.

5.   DOLORES: Think I'll see to the porch first. Use what's left for
      the pews.

REV. COX, SATISFIED WITH HIS DOOR OILING, STARTS
OUT INTO VESTRY.

6.   REV. COX: As you will. I'm going to tackle that vestry locker.
      Stop it sounding like a Hammer Horror.

REV. COX EXITS. DOLORES, NOW ALONE, GIVES WAY
TO FUMING UPSET.

                                            CUT TO:

-24-

<u>Sc. 09 (INT.) STAFFORD SITTING ROOM 11.30</u>

<u>SONIA</u> AND <u>GAVIN</u> HAVE BEEN ARGUING OVER THE TOP OF BRAD'S HEAD AS HE SITS, STILL READING MAGAZINE AND IGNORING THEIR DISPUTE.

1. GAVIN: How many times? I didn't tell the papers. The reporter said he'd heard from a source at the school. And, anyway, it's only the local rag.

2. SONIA: That's all anyone reads around here! And now you've gone and committed yourself in print, how are you going to be able to back down?

3. GAVIN: I'd no intention of backing down – with or without the publicity. (SMUG) Bet you it'll embarrass the school into caving in, though.

4. SONIA: And if it doesn't? How far are you going to take this?

THE PHONE RINGS. <u>SONIA</u> SNATCHES UP THE RECEIVER.

5. SONIA: (IRRITABLY) Yes? Hello? (LISTENS THEN MODERATES HER TONE) Oh. Well, er, thank you. That's great. (LISTENS) Right. Fine. Ten tomorrow then. Bye.

A SLIGHTLY STUNNED <u>SONIA</u> REPLACES THE RECEIVER. SHE LOOKS AT <u>GAVIN</u>, HER ENTHUSIASM QUALIFIED BY THE PROBLEM HE HAS CAUSED.

-25-

1. SONIA: I've got the job.

2. GAVIN: Great! Fantastic. (TAPS <u>BRAD</u> ON THE HEAD) Clever Mum, eh?

3. BRAD: (BRIEFLY LOOKS UP FROM MAGAZINE) Nice one, Ma.

<u>BRAD</u> RETURNS TO READING. <u>SONIA</u> INDICATES THE OBLIVIOUS <u>BRAD</u> BY POINTING AT HIS HEAD.

146

4.   SONIA: (TO <u>GAVIN</u>, MOCK SWEET) Just one small problem, isn't there? Thanks to you.

5.   GAVIN: No, there isn't. If they want you to go in at ten tomorrow to discuss things, that's fine. I can keep an eye on Brad. And then we can set about getting something proper fixed up for when you start.

6.   SONIA: (FLATLY) Gavin. Ten tomorrow <u>is</u> when I start.

<u>SONIA</u> REGARDS <u>GAVIN</u> WITH WRY EXPECTATION.

ON <u>GAVIN</u>, LOST FOR A SOLUTION.

CUT TO:

END OF PART ONE

-26-

<u>Sc. 10   (INT.)   DENTS' KITCHEN   13.00</u>

<u>DESMOND</u> HAS JUST UNWRAPPED A BOXED PEN AND PENCIL SET. HE KISSES <u>PHILIPPA</u> ON THE CHEEK.

1.   DESMOND: Thank you, sweetheart.

2.   PHILIPPA: It's not very original.

<u>DESMOND</u> PICKS UP PEN AND FAKES ENTHUSIASM FOR IT.

3.   DESMOND: I'll have clients queuing up to sign on the dotted with this.

<u>PHILIPPA</u> GOES TO KETTLE AND SWITCHES IT ON. SHE REACHES FOR MUGS, COFFEE AND WILL GET MILK FROM FRIDGE.

4.   PHILIPPA: Want me to fix you some lunch?

5.   DESMOND: (STILL BROODING ABOUT MISSED BIRTHDAY TREAT) No, ta. (A NICE IDEA STRIKES) Hey, since your Mum couldn't – how about you and me popping out for a birthday bite?

6.   PHILIPPA: Grabbed a pizza in the staff canteen. Sorry.

147

-27-

1.   DESMOND: (DISGUISING DISAPPOINTMENT) Yeah, well, another time.

<u>DESMOND</u> PUTS PEN BACK IN BOX THEN WATCHES <u>PHILIPPA</u> MAKE COFFEE. SHE SEEMS DISTRACTED.

2.   DESMOND: It's working out for you, is it? This agency lark?

3.   PHILIPPA: Mmm? Oh, yes. No, it's fine.

4.   DESMOND: Just – your Mum seems to think something's bothering you. You can tell me, you know, if there's anything –

<u>PHILIPPA</u> TAKES UP HER COFFEE MUG AND STARTS OUT OF ROOM.

5.   PHILIPPA: Dad – I'm fine. I just want to get out of my uniform – then I've got to nip out.

ON <u>DESMOND</u> WONDERING IF THERE IS SOMETHING BOTHERING HIS DAUGHTER

                                        CUT TO:

-28-

<u>Sc. 11   (INT.)   HARGROVE BACK BEDROOM   13.10</u>

<u>SUSAN</u> LIES ON HER BED IN THE SEMI-DARK ROOM. SHE IS UNCONSCIOUS. AN EMPTY BOTTLE OF PILLS LIES BY THE BED. NEXT TO IT AN ALMOST EMPTY BOTTLE OF VODKA IS LYING ON ITS SIDE.

DOWNSTAIRS THE TELEPHONE IS RINGING.

ON <u>SUSAN</u>, OBLIVIOUS TO THE CONTINUING RINGING OF THE TELEPHONE

                                        CUT TO:

Sc. 12 (INT.) STAFFORD KITCHEN 13.12

SONIA IS TRYING TO RUB A STAIN OFF A SKIRT. GAVIN IS LOOKING THROUGH HIS TELEPHONE ADDRESS BOOK.

1. SONIA: I'm going to need some new clothes. Still, I'll be able to afford them – now that I'll be earning.

2. GAVIN: (BRIGHT IDEA VIA ADDRESS BOOK) Why don't I ring Maureen? I'm sure she'll keep an eye on Brad for us.

3. SONIA: What, from Ibiza? She's there for the next two weeks, remember?

4. GAVIN: (DEFLATED) I suppose I could take him to the restaurant with me everyday – and you could pick him up on your way home. (THIS NOT A DESIRABLE OPTION, GAVIN GOES BACK TO ADDRESS BOOK) There's got to be somebody.

5. SONIA: (EXITING) Good, because you've got all of half-a-day left to find them.

ON GAVIN'S DILEMMA.

CUT TO:

-30-

Sc. 13 (INT.) BAPTIST CHAPEL 13.15

DOLORES IS ZIPPING UP HER COAT/COLLECTING HER BAG. SHE LOOKS TIGHT-LIPPED IN ANTICIPATION OF TACKLING DESMOND.

REVEREND COX ENTERS FROM VESTRY, DRESSED FOR CONDUCTING WEDDING SERVICE.

1. REV. COX: Thanks a million for stepping in at such short notice, Dolores. (NODDING AT FLOWERS) Or should that be thanks a bunch.

DOLORES MANAGES A SMILE AS SHE STARTS TO
LEAVE.

2.   DOLORES: You're welcome. See you Sunday.

3.   REV. COX: (CALLING AFTER HER) And be sure to give
Desmond my happy birthday wish.

4.   DOLORES: (LIGHT IN TONE, BUT WITH PRIVATE
MENACE) Don't worry – I'll see he gets it.

ON DOLORES, HEADED FOR BATTLE.

CUT TO:

-31-

Sc. 14.   (EXT.)   STREET O/S HARGROVES'   13.30

GREG IS PROPPED AGAINST HIS CAR AS HE LOOKS AT
THE HARGROVE HOUSE, WAITING FOR AN ANSWER
TO HIS MOBILE PHONE-CALL. GETTING NO REPLY, HE
SLAPS THE COVER OF HIS MOBILE SHUT. WONDERING
WHAT TO DO NEXT. GREG SPOTS PHILIPPA LEAVING
THE DENT HOUSE AND CALLS TO HER.

1.   GREG: (IRRITABLE WITH FRUSTRATION) Don't suppose
you've seen Susan, have you?

2.   PHILIPPA: (IRONICALLY) And a very good afternoon to you
too, Greg. Lost your PA, have you?

3.   GREG: I've been round here twice – and back to the office in
case she'd turned up. I can't think where else she could have
got to.

4.   PHILIPPA: (KEEPS WALKING/SHRUGS) Maybe she's given
herself the day off to go shopping or something. It is
Independence Day.

ON GREG NOT APPRECIATING THE HUMOUR AND
WONDERING WORRIEDLY WHAT TO DO NEXT.

CUT TO:

-32-

<u>Sc. 15 (INT.) CUTZ SALON 13.35</u>

<u>NICOLA</u> IS RINSING PERM ROLLERS AT A BACK-WASH BASIN. <u>DEBRA</u> IS BLOW-DRYING A CLIENT'S HAIR. SHE CALLS OVER TO <u>NICOLA</u>.

1.   DEBRA: Mousse, if you please, Nicola.

<u>NICOLA</u> SIGHS, DRIES HER HANDS AND GOES TO THE COUNTER ONLY A YARD OR SO AWAY FROM WHERE <u>DEBRA</u> IS WORKING. SHE HANDS THE CAN OF MOUSSE TO <u>DEBRA</u> WHO GIVES A TIGHT SMILE BY WAY OF THANKS. <u>NICOLA</u> IS ON HER WAY BACK TO HER CHORE WHEN <u>PHILIPPA</u> ENTERS.

<u>DEBRA</u> CALLS TO <u>PHILIPPA</u> ASSUMING SHE IS A CLIENT.

2.   DEBRA: Bear with me. Be with you in a mo!

<u>NICOLA</u> HEADS TOWARDS <u>PHILIPPA</u> WHO HOVERS BY RECEPTION.

3.   NICOLA: It's all-right, Mrs Thorn. It's a friend of mine.

4.   DEBRA: (POINTEDLY) Goodness, you are popular.

-33-

<u>PHILIPPA</u> SEES SHE'S PUT <u>NICOLA</u> IN AN AWKWARD POSITION. BOTH KEEP THEIR VOICES DOWN. <u>DEBRA</u> WILL EYE THEM DISAPPROVINGLY THROUGHOUT.

1.   PHILIPPA: Sorry. Just wondered what time you got off.

2.   NICOLA: Half-five. A life sentence.

3.   PHILIPPA: You couldn't meet me, could you? I need to talk to you about what I should do.

4.   NICOLA: But you already know what I think. I can't believe you haven't just told them and got it over with.

151

5.   PHILIPPA: Mum'll freak, though. And as for Dad. . .
(ENVISAGES HIS BAD REACTION)

6.   NICOLA: You don't know that 'til you give them a chance.
They might be okay about it.

7.   PHILIPPA: Yeah – right. Pillars of the chapel and straighter
than a couple of pokers – they're bound to go for it big style.

-34-

1.   DEBRA: (SUGAR-COATED) If it's not blighting your social
life too much, Nicola – I will be needing the spray-and-shine.

NICOLA, WITH HER BACK TO DEBRA, GRIMACES AND
THEN ANSWERS SWEETLY.

2.   NICOLA: Be right there, Mrs Thorn. (THEN TO PHILIPPA)
Just tell them. And nip round later – let me know how it went.

PHILIPPA NODS UNCERTAINLY. NICOLA HEADS OFF TO
FIND HAIRSPRAY. ON PHILIPPA TRYING TO SUMMON
SOME DETERMINATION.

                           CUT TO:

-35-

<u>Sc. 16   (EXT.)   DENT REAR PATIO   13.40</u>

DOLORES, RECENTLY ARRIVED HOME AND STILL
WEARING JACKET, IS FURIOUS WITH DESMOND.
DESMOND DISGUISES GUILT BY SHEDDING HIS
GARDENING GLOVES.

1.   DOLORES: I can't believe you could have been so two-faced!

DESMOND PUTS GLOVES ON PATIO TABLE. HE KEEPS
HIS VOICE DOWN.

2.   DESMOND: And I can't believe you'd even think such a thing.

3.   DOLORES: Oh, don't you come the wounded saint with me,
you ... (SNATCHES UP GARDENING GLOVES AND SWIPES
HIM ACROSS THE FACE WITH THEM) ... You hypocrite!!

DESMOND, ALTHOUGH SHOCKED, IS AWARE OF THEIR
NON-PRIVATE SURROUNDINGS.

4. DESMOND: Dolores, please – not out here.

-36-

1. DOLORES: Why not?! I should be the one who's worried
    about people knowing! I'm the fool whose husband is cheating
    on her. Messing about with a girl young enough to be his
    daughter!

2. DESMOND: But it isn't true!

3. DOLORES: Oh, really? Well, we'll see about that. (STARTS
    INTO HOUSE) We'll just see what Little Miss Hargrove has to
    say about it, shall we?

4. DESMOND: (PANICKING) No!

DOLORES RUNS INTO THE HOUSE.

ON DESMOND, MOMENTARILY ROOTED BY PANIC.

CUT TO:

-37-

Sc. 17.   (EXT.)   STREET O/S HARGROVES'   13.44

GREG HAS JUST GOT BACK INTO HIS CAR AND IS
SHUTTING THE DRIVER'S DOOR. ABOUT TO START THE
IGNITION HE SEES A DISTRESSED DOLORES COMING
OUT OF DENT HOUSE. GREG WATCHES DOLORES
CROSS TO THE HARGROVE FRONT DOOR. GREG
LOWERS THE WINDOW AND WATCHES AS AN ANXIOUS
DESMOND APPEARS IN PURSUIT OF HIS WIFE.
INTRIGUED, GREG GETS OUT OF THE CAR AND HEADS
TOWARDS DOLORES WHO IS PRESSING THE HARGROVE
DOOR BELL AND THEN KNOCKING URGENTLY.

1. GREG: Is there a problem?

2. (DESMOND ARRIVES BEFORE DOLORES CAN
    RESPOND) No. No, problem at all. Dolores has just got the
    wrong idea –

153

3. DOLORES: I don't think so. (RINGS DOORBELL AGAIN)
    But I'm sure Susan will enlighten me.

4. GREG: (BEWILDERED) But she isn't in. I've been trying to
    find her all day.

    DOLORES BELIEVES HIM FOR A SECOND AND THEN
    LOOKS FROM <u>GREG</u> TO A RELIEVED <u>DESMOND</u> – AND
    BACK AT <u>GREG</u> AGAIN WITH A CYNICAL SMILE – SHE
    SMELLS A CONSPIRACY.

-38-

1. DOLORES: Oh, I get it. All men together. I'd expect you to
    take his side.

2. GREG: About what? I don't even know what . . . (IS GOING
    ON)

3. DOLORES: Oh, come on, Greg. You're not telling me you
    didn't know your precious PA was having an affair.

4. GREG: (SHOCKED LOOK AT DESMOND) It was <u>you</u>?
    (LOOKS DISGUSTED)

5. DESMOND: No! Why won't anybody believe me?

6. DOLORES: (EVENLY) Because we've been here before,
    haven't we, Des? (LIFTS HAND TO RING DOORBELL
    AGAIN) That's why I need to hear it from Susan.

    <u>DESMOND</u> CATCHES <u>DOLORES</u>' HAND BEFORE SHE
    CAN RING THE BELL AGAIN.

7. DESMOND: No, don't. (QUIETLY ADMITTING) All right.
    We . . . saw each other. A couple of times. But nothing
    happened. And, anyway, it's over.

    <u>DOLORES</u> LOOKS SCEPTICAL. <u>GREG</u> LOOKS WORRIED.

-39-

1. GREG: Since when?

    <u>DESMOND</u> IS FROZEN BY <u>DOLORES</u>' CONTEMPT.

154

2.   GREG: (SHOUTING) I said, since when was it over?!

3.   DESMOND: (STARTLED) Since yesterday. (TO <u>DOLORES</u>) I
      realised what a fool I was being. I wanted it finished before my
      birthday – a clean start . . .

UNCEREMONIOUSLY, <u>GREG</u> PUSHES BETWEEN
<u>DESMOND</u> AND <u>DOLORES</u> TO GET TO THE FRONT
DOOR. THEY WATCH, STUNNED, AS <u>GREG</u> HITS A
GLASS DOOR PANE WITH HIS ELBOW AND SMASHES IT.

4.   DOLORES: What're you doing!?

<u>GREG</u> REACHES THROUGH THE BROKEN PANE AND
STRUGGLES TO UNLOCK THE DOOR.

5.   GREG: (TO <u>DESMOND</u>) If she's hurt herself because of you
      . . .! (MURDEROUS GLARE)

6.   DESMOND: (FEEBLY) Don't be ridiculous. She wouldn't –

-40-

<u>GREG</u> THROWS OPEN THE DOOR AND RUSHES INTO
THE HOUSE, CALLING FRANTICALLY AS HE MOVES
DOWN THE HALLWAY TOWARDS THE STAIRS.

1.   GREG: Susan? Susan!?

FROM <u>DESMOND/DOLORES</u>' POV WE SEE <u>GREG</u> RUN
UP THE STAIRS. <u>DOLORES</u> LOOKS AT <u>DESMOND</u> WITH
A MIXTURE OF CONTEMPT AND DISBELIEF. <u>DESMOND</u>,
ASHAMED, LOOKS AWAY. <u>DOLORES</u> NOW HURRIES
INTO THE HOUSE AND UP THE STAIRS.

ON <u>DESMOND</u>'S EXPRESSION OF DAWNING DREAD.

CUT TO:

-41-

<u>Sc. 18   (INT.)   CUTZ SALON   13.55</u>

<u>DEBRA</u> IS ENTERING AN APPOINTMENT IN THE BOOK.
AN UNHAPPY AND ANNOYED <u>NICOLA</u> IS STANDING

BY THE DESK. A CLIENT SITS IN THE BACKGROUND, READING A MAGAZINE.

1.   NICOLA: But tomorrow's my college morning.

2.   DEBRA: Not this week, I'm afraid. I can find too much use for you here.

3.   NICOLA: (ANGER MOUNTING) Yeah, as a skivvy. (THEN TRYING TO REASON) I could be <u>really</u> useful to you if I can just get through my training.

4.   DEBRA: (UNMOVED) Yes, well, all in good time. Tomorrow I need you here.

<u>DEBRA</u> STARTS TO MOVE AWAY FROM DESK, BUT <u>NICOLA</u> STOPS HER WITH A SHOUT.

5.   NICOLA: No! It's not fair!

-42-

1.   DEBRA: (*SOTTO VOCE* TO <u>NICOLA</u>) We'll discuss this later.

<u>DEBRA</u> MOVES TOWARDS CLIENT. FUMING, <u>NICOLA</u> OVERTAKES HER AND SWEEPS PAST INTO THE STOCKROOM.

2.   DEBRA: (TO CLIENT AND AS SHE ASSESSES PROGRESS OF COLOUR TREATMENT) Oh, yes. That's going to come out lovely for you.

<u>NICOLA</u> SWEEPS BACK OUT OF STOCKROOM, HAVING GATHERED UP SWEATER AND BAG. <u>DEBRA</u> WATCHES INCREDULOUSLY AS <u>NICOLA</u> HEADS FOR THE SALON DOOR.

3.   DEBRA: Excuse me? Is there something I've missed?

<u>NICOLA</u> HALTS BY THE RECEPTION DESK AND TURNS TO <u>DEBRA</u> WITH AN IRONIC SMILE.

4.   NICOLA: You've missed the chance of having somebody dead keen like me working for you.

NICOLA PICKS AN AMERICAN FLAG FROM THE DISPLAY
ON THE DESK AND WAVES IT MOCKINGLY AT DEBRA.

-43-

1.   NICOLA: Bye!

NICOLA STARTS TO EXIT. BEHIND HER SHE LEAVES AN
ASTOUNDED DEBRA AND FASCINATED CLIENT. ON A
TRIMPHANT NICOLA.

CUT TO:

-44-

Sc. 19   (EXT.)   DENTS' REAR PATIO   14.00

SIMON IS STANDING AT THE EDGE OF THE PATIO
WITH HIS BACK TO CAMERA. TENSE, HE RUNS HIS
HAND THROUGH HIS HAIR. PHILIPPA'S VOICE MAKES
HIM START AND TURN.

1.   PHILIPPA: Here you go.

2.   SIMON: (STARTLED, THEN SEES MUG OF TEA SHE IS
     HOLDING OUT TO HIM) Oh, thanks. Thought they were here.

3.   PHILIPPA: They must have gone out for Dad's birthday lunch
     after all. (TENSE NOW) They'll probably be back soon.

4.   SIMON: (HESITANT) Do you ... ? Do you think we really
     need to tell them ... everything?

5.   PHILLIPA: (SHRUGS BUT NOT RELISHING THE
     THOUGHT) May as well get hung for a sheep as a lamb.

PHILIPPA ATTEMPTS AN ENCOURAGING SMILE BUT IT
IS RATHER WEAK. SIMON TRIES A RETURN SMILE BUT
IT QUICKLY DISSOLVES BACK INTO APPREHENSION.
ON THE NERVOUS PAIR.

CUT TO:

157

-45-

Sc. 20   (EXT.)   STREET O/S HARGROVES'   14.10

GREG IS STANDING BY THE AMBULANCE DOOR. FROM
HIS POV WE SEE AMBULANCEMAN ADJUSTING
BLANKET OVER SUSAN WHO LIES INSIDE AMBULANCE
WEARING OXYGEN MASK. BEHIND GREG, DESMOND
AND DOLORES WATCH FROM THE BOTTOM OF THEIR
DRIVEWAY. GREG TURNS AT THE SOUND OF NICOLA'S
VOICE AS SHE APPROACHES.

1.   NICOLA: (ALARMED) Greg!? What's going on?

NICOLA REACHES THE AMBULANCE DOOR AND
LOOKS IN TO SEE HER SISTER.

2.   NICOLA: Suze!? (SHE LOOKS AT GREG)

3.   GREG: An overdose.

NICOLA LOOKS BEWILDERED. GREG DOESN'T WANT
TO CAUSE DELAY WHILE HE EXPLAINS.

4.   GREG: You go with her. I'll follow on in the car.

-46-

NICOLA STARTS TO GET INTO THE AMBULANCE AND
THEN LOOKS BACK AT GREG.

1.   NICOLA: But she is going to be all right?

GREG DOESN'T KNOW. THE AMBULANCEMAN LEANS
OVER TO CLOSE THE DOOR. BEHIND GREG, A
TEARFUL DOLORES TURNS AND STARTS TOWARDS
THE HOUSE. DESMOND'S CONTRITE ATTENTION TO
SUSAN'S FATE NOW TURNS TO DOLORES WHO HE
BEGINS TO FOLLOW.

2.   DESMOND: Doll . . .

DOLORES IGNORES HIM AND GOES ON TOWARDS THE
HOUSE.

ON <u>GREG</u>'S WORRIED EXPRESSION AS THE
AMBULANCE DRIVES AWAY.

CUT TO:

-47-

<u>Sc. 21   (INT.)   STAFFORD SITTING ROOM   14.12</u>

<u>GAVIN</u> IS AT THE FRONT WINDOW TRYING TO SEE
OUT AT AN ANGLE. <u>SONIA</u> ENTERS/WILL HEAD
TOWARDS PHONE.

1.   GAVIN: Ambulance. Can't see what's going on.

2.   SONIA: (DOESN'T CARE/PICKS UP PHONE) I'll just have
to ring them, that's all. Tell them I can't start tomorrow.

3.   GAVIN: (PLEASED WITH HIMSELF) No, it's fine. I've sorted
Sarah out to come and look after Brad.

4.   SONIA: (HAS TO THINK THEN IT DAWNS) Sarah the
waitress? But she's not much older than him.

5.   GAVIN: (CONFIDENT) Trust me, it'll be fine.

<u>GAVIN</u> TURNS BACK TO WINDOW. <u>SONIA</u> HESITATES
BEFORE REPLACING THE TELEPHONE RECEIVER AND
THEN DOES SO. ON <u>SONIA</u>'S LINGERING
RESERVATIONS.

CUT TO:

-48-

<u>Sc. 22   (INT.)   DENT KITCHEN   14.15</u>

<u>PHILIPPA</u> IS RINSING COFFEE MUG AT THE SINK.
<u>SIMON</u> IS FINISHING HIS COFFEE AND ALMOST
CHOKES ON IT AS THEY HEAR THE FRONT DOOR
OPEN AND SHUT.

1.   PHILIPPA: At least they should be in a good mood.

<u>PHILIPPA</u> AND <u>SIMON</u> SHARE WOBBLY CONFIDENCE-
INSPIRING SMILES.

159

2. DOLORES: (OOV) (ANGRILY) I don't want to hear it,
    Desmond!

    PHILIPPA AND SIMON EXCHANGE LESS CONFIDENT
    GLANCES. DOLORES APPEARS IN KITCHEN DOORWAY
    AND STOPS DEAD IN HER TRACKS AT FINDING A
    STRANGER WITH HER DAUGHTER.

3. PHILIPPA: (LAMELY) Hi, Mum. This is, er, Simon.

    DOLORES ATTEMPTS A POLITE EXPRESSION.
    DESMOND ENTERS AND, SEEING THE UNKNOWN
    YOUNG MAN, LOOKS EQUALLY BAFFLED.

4. DOLORES: Well, er, hello there. Always nice to meet a friend
    of Philippa's.

                            -49-

1. PHILIPPA: (TO DESMOND) Dad, this is Simon. (JOKING
    FEEBLY) And, er, actually, we're kind of more than just good
    friends, as they say.

2. DESMOND: (NOT SURE HE APPROVES) Oh?

3. DOLORES: (SURPRISED BUT PLEASED AND
    ADDRESSING HERSELF TO SIMON) This is typical of her.
    Dark horse if ever there was one.

    THERE IS AN AWKWARD MOMENT WHERE EVERYONE
    IS TRYING TO BE PLEASANT, BUT NO-ONE KNOWS
    WHAT TO SAY.

4. PHILIPPA: I'm sorry this is springing it on you both, but . . .
    there's something I – we – have to tell you. And it can't really
    wait any longer.

5. DESMOND: (WEARILY) Oh, no.

6. PHILIPPA: (REALISING HE THINKS SHE IS PREGNANT
    AND AMUSED) Dad! No! I'm not pregnant, if that's what
    you're thinking.

    DESMOND AND DOLORES LOOK RELIEVED.

7.   DOLORES: (FIBBING) Well, I knew you'd more sense than that.

-50-

1.   SIMON: (BRAVELY) What Philippa's trying to tell you is that . . . we've decided to move in together.

2.   DESMOND: (HEAVY FATHER) Now just hang on a minute. . .

3.   DOLORES: Oh, for pity's sake, Des – she is twenty-two. It's what people do nowadays. They don't rush into getting married.

4.   PHILIPPA: (HESITANTLY) Well, actually, we would if we could. What I mean is, that's the other thing you should know. (TAKES SIMON'S HAND FOR COURAGE) Simon's already married.

5.   SIMON: But I'll be getting a divorce!

DESMOND, DESPONDENT, SLUMPS DOWN ONTO A KITCHEN CHAIR. DOLORES LOOKS DOWN AT HER HUSBAND, HOPING THAT THE IRONY IS PAINFUL.

6.   PHILIPPA: (WANTING MUM'S UNDERSTANDING) Mum?

7.   DOLORES: Oh, I think this is one for your father. I'm sure he's got a lot to say about married men and affairs.

-51-

PHILIPPA LOOKS PERPLEXED.

DESMOND SHOOTS DOLORES A PANICKED LOOK THAT PLEADS FOR HER NOT TO TELL. PHILIPPA, SIMON AND DOLORES ALL WAIT FOR WHAT HE HAS TO SAY. ON DESMOND LOOKING HUNTED.

CUT TO:

END OF EPISODE

12. And the Next Exciting Episode?

It has been said that everything is becoming a Soap. The serial or 'strip' (as in strip-cartoon) programme structure, with its reliance on the The Hook device, increasingly underpins all manner of television's output – from advertisements, through drama-documentary to what have become unashamedly labelled Docu-Soaps. Elements of The Hook can even be detected in some news bulletins that flag upcoming items in such a way as to entice the viewer to stay with the programme.

When it comes to drama, most of what's available on the small screen is offered up in bites numbering anywhere from two to a season-long run. Whereas, at one time, only adaptations of classics and one or two medical and police dramas were served up serial-fashion, it is now rare for any drama to appear as a single, separate piece. Where yesteryear's most distinguished or best burgeoning writing talents were the natural source of the single television play, their contemporary counterparts are now, on the whole, more accustomed to having their work presented in a serialised form.

Whether this be good, bad or irrelevant in terms of writing standards has been the subject of much debate. There is, though, a general recognition that this trend towards 'strip' television is more a corporate than a creatively inspired change of tack.

As the number of television channels increased and competition grew, programme-providers needed more of their output to not only attract viewers but also keep them faithful. And not only must any drama be a sure-fire audience winner with designs on winning the audience back week after week – it must be relatively cheap to produce. Since Soap had, from its inception, been so successfully managing to fulfil all of these remits, it's hardly surprising that programme-providers looked to its well-proven formula and saw it as the way to go.

162

For what it's worth, I believe that the increasing tendency to see it as the *only* way to go has already led to an impoverishment. Although the occasional serialised drama on our screens still manages to circumvent the tendency for the formulaic, there is too much that doesn't. The single drama was, and still is, the only place where original formulae bearing a truly unique slant can be created. It is the realisation of an individual writer's imagination.

Just as the short story exists as a form in its own right – an entity which can't be stretched without it becoming something entirely different, i.e. a novel – single drama has a thrust and symmetry all of its own. Designed as a single stab at the heart, mind or guts, much of its power and passion lies in its very distillation. As a self-contained, short, sharp lunge it can carry the added shock-tactic of surprise. To draw it out is to dilute its strength, intensity and intent.

The single television play as we once knew it is already long beyond being an endangered species. It is now so rare that too much rests on the success of what little there is. As in publishing, where the novel list has been reduced to a handful of high-profile authors whose sales guarantee huge returns, so nervous, result-driven television programme-providers have become less and less inclined to take a risk on single plays from anyone but the most established writers.

Some of the disappointed playwrights-in-the-proper-sense find their way through to writing serial drama, and others turn up to enrich Soap-writing teams; but I suspect many original and innovative voices have never been allowed to reach us above the unholy clamour to turn all drama into a sort of Soap.

As for the Soap genre itself, much has been written and said about its quality and importance. As to quality, some Soaps are slated for falling short on taste and integrity almost all of the time, while others fall from critical favour only some of the time. At its best, Soap has provided some of the most memorable television moments ever. At its worst, in its laxest and most lunatic moments, it has delivered a depth of dross which is best forgotten.

Good, poor or putrid, whether, ultimately, any of it matters is perhaps a more crucial question. If Soap does, as some claim, reflect the society we live in, then it follows that it matters how accurately or distortedly that picture is refracted back to us. If, as others believe, Soap has the power not only to show but to actually shape and influence our society in its values, views and behaviour, it needs to be taken very seriously indeed.

Among the claims made for it, Soap has been called 'the soul of the nation', more powerful than politics in the way it can influence and even change our attitudes to social and moral issues. Indeed, Government itself has lent credence to Soap's own sense of importance. When, as Prime Minister, Tony Blair lightheartedly called for the release of an imprisoned Soap character, he was, consciously or not, proving more than his own desire to be populist. By identifying with the Soap-watching public, he was not only acknowledging Soap as an acceptable preoccupation of the masses, but also reinforcing the Soap Tsars' own claim that their product is more than mere entertainment – that it could enter and impact on an electorate's reality. Having made this tacit acknowledgement that Soap had superceded secular and religious authority in the lives of many, it's no surprise that the government went on to conscript Soap as a propoganda tool in, for instance, their drive to promote reading.

As to the Soaps themselves, they increasingly insinuate into reality and assert their own credentials as public informers and educators by running details of real-life help-lines at the close of episodes of drama. This bleeding over the line between the dilemmas faced by fictional characters into what real-life members of the audience may be experiencing is fast becoming the norm. It is used especially with episodes written around painful and isolating problems such as racism, rape, drugs, dyslexia, Aids, abuse, alcholism, anorexia, homophobia, etc.

While the intent may be a basically good one, the line gets blurred even further when actors become involved outside their soap role with lobbying or raising the profile of a particular issue. When actors and producers, as they increasingly do, pop up in the press or on radio and TV to add their voices to a debate on some serious issue, it could be seen to be implying a weight of authority on the subject. It might even be said that by touting and spouting about an issue their own show has contrived to make topical, Soap, rather than any social or moral imperative, is setting the agenda.

Not that it is new for Soap to be used to inform and educate: the radio series *The Archers* was actually conceived as a vehicle for communicating information to the farming population, and many overseas governments have promulgated health and welfare programmes via popular drama. Soap can be the most effective – and sometimes the only – way to reach huge and geographically scattered populations in poorer countries.

But a more recent and novel claim that has been made for Soap in our own country is that it is the only shared experience we have left. With the splintering of the family unit and the disintegration of communities as we once knew them, Soap Operas have, one television executive asserted, become the sole remaining uniting force.

A force for good? According to the same exec, most certainly so, especially in the way Soaps have unified a nation which, without them, would be as divided as ever by social and class structures. 'Soaps,' this same advocate said, 'set out to reflect society, but end up affecting, gently changing, the way we think about our lives, and those around us.'

It was an idea that author Fay Weldon reacted strongly against: 'Soaps may well be better for us than Valium – they're certainly easier on the liver – but they are still an alternative to life, not part of it. Soaps become the centre of people's lives but it is truly a miserable and ghastly life without a single laugh or aspiration. Characters in Soap Operas are appalling role-models providing an extraordinarily narrow view of human reaction with an emotional and political correctness which ends up narrowing our lives rather than expanding them.'

Guardian television reviewer Nancy Banks-Smith took one of her traditionally amusing but insightful sideswipes at the Soap genre which amounted to much the same thing: 'In *EastEnders* you are most likely to sleep with your mother-in-law or the vicar. In *Brookside* most likely to explode in a power shower while making love to a plumber. In *Coronation Street* to marry Ken Barlow and in *The Archers* to have millennium twins. Soap Operas do our dirty washing for us. They save us the bother of loving our neighbour or having sex with the plumber. And personally I couldn't be more grateful.'

The reality of how differently Soap is perceived and received into people's lives probably lies somewhere in the middle of these two extremes. And yet, even with its importance relegated to this degree, it has clearly become a force to be reckoned with.

When, on average, our four best-known Soaps can collectively command anywhere between 37 and 52 million viewers, we have to take the genre seriously. When the genre-providers see themselves as social engineers it is even more crucial that we monitor their fitness for the role.

As with any message, we the audience need to ask who is sending it and why? If programme-makers hold themseves to be capable of tinkering with our values and instrumental in the forming of our opinions, they should also be accountable. Unfortunately, in my experience, accountability comes and goes in the corridors of The-Powers-That-Be. When seen to be on the side of the angels for having delivered a responsible storyline that inspires informed debate, Soap bosses fall over themselves to collect the accolades. However, given viewer or critical reaction *against* their output over some questionable moral or social message, Soap bosses can't wash their hands quickly enough. The mantle of self-professed purveyors of brilliant, iconic telly is cast off in a shrug: 'How can they take us so seriously, for God's sake? It's ONLY television!'

Soap-makers may forget that as and when it suits, but as long as we the audience remember it – as I'm convinced most of us do – I think we're safe to go on enjoying our Soaps. Just as I am convinced that the vast majority of us live our lives around Soap, not through them. This I maintain because, while there is more Soap of all sorts on our screen, the overall television viewing trend is downwards. For the anti-misanthropes amongst us, this means subscribing to the theory that television *per se* is totally irrelevant to some, as well as being so much less central than it was to those who continue to watch it. There may well be a TV in every room of the house, and all of them may be on all of the time, but, for whole hosts of the population, they could constitute little more than illustrated 'muzak' against which the real business of relating, rearing families, housework and hobbies is played out.

Among the growing myriad of little screen experiences – the computer, the email, the Web on which we can shop, bank and access a world's worth of information – television becomes just another piece of pixelation. Just a part of our experience, not an experience in itself, and nowhere near as influential a one as when we huddled hushed in the reverential dark while the box in the corner spake its wisdom and revealed its miracles unto us.

True, for the lost, lonely and terminally lazy, television provides all too easy a distraction. And, let's face it, there are times when all any of us want is chewing-gum for the eyes. But when we worry about a new generation being trapped in the box's thrall to a physically and mentally damaging degree, we should perhaps ourselves be looking beyond television for the cause. And the blame. Television could not in itself create an easily mollified, under-educated, directionless, junk-fed generation. We, as a society, did that.

If it is true that so many people feel dislocated and isolated to the point where the second-hand Soap neighbourhood seems like the only safe and interesting place for them to unite, we, as a society, should be setting about creating them a better real community.

But enough with the diatribe. While we can argue about the influence and importance of television in general and Soaps in particular, there is no disputing how many more Soap Operas there are on our screens. The worst-case scenario is that, in an effort to outdo each other, they will all abandon character and story development in favour of expensive stunts and cheap thrills. In the best of all worlds, the proliferation would lead to even fiercer competition which, ultimately, would lead to a better overall standard of product that allowed writers the chance to create worthwhile popular drama.

As to the mixed bag of Soap Opera that's currently on offer, there is a case for saying that, like an electorate gets the government it deserves, we as viewers get the Soaps we deserve. The difference is that when Soap is serving us badly or trying to manipulate us in ways we don't like, we don't even have to get off the couch to get rid of it.

What comes next in the world of Soaps is only in part up to the producers and writers. More crucially, it is up to us as viewers to call the shots on quality. If the viewing figures for sub-standard Soaps fall, programme-makers will eventually respond by offering us something more thoughtful and thought-provoking. After all, we only have to lift a finger to exercise the power we have over it –

We can vote with the remote.

Index